Cultural Violence, Stigma the Legacy of the Anti-Sealing Movement

This book injects nuance into the debate about the moral legitimacy of environmental and animal activism and explores how activism can lead to stigma and destruction of minority group identities, cultural practices and community structures. It takes readers back to ground zero of the anti-sealing movement – Newfoundland and Labrador. This book sheds light on the human costs of activism and the repercussions for vulnerable people when activists normalize forms of violence as acceptable to achieve their desired outcomes.

Inspired by Greenpeace Canada's apology to Canadian Inuit, Indigenous and coastal peoples, this book brings into focus the local peoples who were targeted by activists and media outlets and left behind once the cultural and economic structures of the sealing industry and sealing practices were severely damaged by activist stigmatization and the global outcry against rural and coastal peoples and their practices.

Drawing upon literature on cultural violence and archival research, this book will be of interest to scholars and researchers of international relations, development studies, public policy, sustainability studies and Indigenous studies.

Danita Catherine Burke is a research fellow at the Center for War Studies, University of Southern Denmark. She has a PhD from the Department of International Politics at Aberystwyth University in Wales, UK, and graduate degrees in Political Science from Memorial University of Newfoundland. Dr. Burke's research has been supported by funding from EU Horizon 2020, the J.R. Smallwood Foundation for Newfoundland and Labrador Studies and the Institute for Advanced Studies in the Humanities (IASH), University of Edinburgh.

Cultural Violence, Stigma and the Legacy of the Anti-Sealing Movement

Danita Catherine Burke

Routledge
Taylor & Francis Group
LONDON AND NEW YORK

First published 2023
by Routledge
4 Park Square, Milton Park, Abingdon, Oxon OX14 4RN

and by Routledge
605 Third Avenue, New York, NY 10158

Routledge is an imprint of the Taylor & Francis Group, an informa business

© 2023 Danita Catherine Burke

British Library Cataloguing-in-Publication Data
A catalogue record for this book is available from the British Library

ISBN: 978-1-032-39790-0 (hbk)
ISBN: 978-1-032-43394-3 (pbk)
ISBN: 978-1-003-35615-8 (ebk)

DOI: 10.4324/9781003356158

Typeset in Times New Roman
by Deanta Global Publishing Services, Chennai, India

Contents

Acknowledgements

I would like to acknowledge and thank my funders. The book was researched and written with the primary funding support of the J.R. Smallwood Foundation for Newfoundland and Labrador Studies (2020–2022). Additional research included in this book was completed while supported by a Horizon 2020 Marie Skłodowska-Curie Individual Fellowship (2018–2020), and edits to the book were completed while supported by a Northern Scholars Visiting Research Fellowship from the Institute for Advanced Studies in the Humanities, University of Edinburgh (2022–2023).

Additionally, I would like to thank my host institutions, namely the Center for War Studies and the Department of Political Science and Public Management, University of Southern Denmark and the Institute for Advanced Studies in the Humanities, University of Edinburgh for their support. Special thanks in particular to Lesley McAra, Pauline Clark and Ben Fletcher-Watson of IASH, Signe Pihl-Thingvad, Vincent Keating and all my colleagues at the Center for War Studies and the International Politics section of the Department of Political Science and Public Management.

Many thanks as well to the interviewees referenced in this book, most notably Anne Troake and James Winter. The interviews with Troake and Winter add their very personal reflections of being on the receiving end and witnessing anti-sealing protest violence in an effort to help provide some balance to the prevailing discourse surrounding sealing, sealing cultures and the anti-sealing cause.

Lastly, this book is also informed by archival research from the Center for Newfoundland Studies (CNS) collected in Spring–Summer 2020 and secondary research from the Ferriss Hodgett Library, Memorial University of Newfoundland and Labrador (MUNL). Special thanks to Colleen Field for her help, and that of her colleagues, with data collection at the CNS and to Nicole Holloway of the Ferriss Hodgett Library, Grenfell Campus, MUN for their assistance in accessing library resources during the Covid-19 lockdown restrictions.

Introduction

The movement against the Canadian/Newfoundland seal hunt by environmentalists and animal rights groups started in the early 20th century and continues to this day, but arguably reached its height in the late 1970s–1980s.
To some organizations, such as the International Fund for Animal Welfare
(IFAW), the People for the Ethical Treatment of Animals (PETA), and Sea
Shepherd Conservation Society and their supporters, their work to undermine
the sealing industry and to highlight their perceived wrongs with sealing practices is a source of pride and accomplishment (e.g. IFAW 2019; PETA 2017;
also see Phelps Bondaroff and Burke 2014). Many organizations involved in
anti-sealing activism, past and present, pushed for the end of commercial seal
hunting and, in some cases, almost all seal hunting (thought eventually many
made an overt caveat for traditional Indigenous subsistence hunting) (e.g.
Allen 1979; Woods 1986; Phelps Bondaroff and Burke 2014). According to
Mark Nuttall (1990, 240) "Animal rights groups have frequently depended on
public opinion for the success of their anti-sealing campaigns, but little sympathy has been shown for the people for whom such opposition has precipitated cultural disintegration". There are cracks now, however, in the legacy of
the anti-sealing activism which invite pause and consideration for the cultural
harms it has caused and continues to cause.[1]

Sealing has been practised most prominently throughout rural and isolated
parts of Canada, most notably, but not exclusively, in parts of the Canadian
Arctic and the Northeast in coastal communities in Newfoundland and
Labrador, the Quebec North Shore and the Magdalen Islands by Indigenous
and non-Indigenous peoples for hundreds, and in some cases thousands,
of years (Sinclair et al. 1989; Burke 2021c; Farquhar 2020; Hawkins and
Silver 2017).[2] Using the case of seal hunting in the Canadian province of
Newfoundland and Labrador, this book argues that the protracted anti-sealing
activism, which has involved many environmental and animal rights organizations and their supporters over the decades, has collectively contributed to
the infliction of cultural violence against Newfoundland and Labrador sealers,
their families and communities, and by extension has also harmed and undermined Indigenous self-determination through limiting sustainable economic
growth for seal products by caging Indigenous nations into a pre-ordained

DOI: 10.4324/9781003356158-1

and limited category of traditional subsistence hunting. As such, this book explores the question, how can the literature on cultural violence and stigma help us understand the experience of the 50 plus years of the anti-sealing campaigning on sealers, their families and coastal communities in Newfoundland and Labrador from the local perspective?

The book makes the case study that the Newfoundland and Labrador experience, particularly those of rural and coastal fishers/sealers, their families and communities at the hands of anti-sealing campaigners (organizations, activists and their supporters), has amounted to cultural violence. In making this case, the book seeks to push scholarly consideration about perpetrators of cultural violence beyond state-centric actors and to acknowledge the growing power and influence of non-state actors, focusing here on environmental and animal rights activist organizations. In pushing for this consideration, the book hopes to foster critical thought about the power of activist organizations in Western society; the scope and impact of colonial actions, attitudes and behaviours in environmental and animal rights activism; and the need for greater awareness about the interconnectedness of long-established Indigenous and non-Indigenous cultures and traditional economic practices in Canada to foster greater accountability for activist organizations so they more fully consider and account for the impacts and potential externalities of their campaigns.

Furthermore, despite Newfoundland and Labrador being ground zero of the anti-sealing campaigning, research into the negative impact of this activism tends to give more focus on the Inuit/Indigenous experiences and economic impacts without adequate acknowledgement or exploration of the depth of the negative experience on traditional, but not exclusively Indigenous, sealing communities (e.g. Hawkins and Silver 2017; Burke 2020; Farquhar 2020). The book argues, therefore, some of the critical scholarship and activist and media discourse on the anti-sealing protests is problematic in two key ways.

First, there is arguably a tendency, in this author's view, for the Newfoundland and Labrador experiences and cultural connections to sealing practices, and those of non-Indigenous sealers in general, tend to be minimized. This is illustrated, for example, by Greenpeace's 2014 apology to Inuit, Indigenous and coastal peoples which emphasizes the organization's impact on Indigenous peoples, particularly Inuit, but provides little substance about their impact on, and contrition toward, coastal non-Indigenous sealers, their families and communities (Kerr 2014). Further indication of efforts to skirt acknowledgement of non-Indigenous cultural connections to sealing is the framing of subsistence sealing as an Inuit/Indigenous cultural activity (e.g. The Canadian Press 2014; Wilkin 1998; Wenzel 1987), excluding traditional subsistence practices by non-Indigenous people, and imposing the image of the "legitimate way to hunt is that symbolised by the Noble Savage, or rather the 'Noble [Inuit]' dressed in furs and hunting seals with a harpoon" (Nuttall 1990, 241).

Second, our ability to comprehend and investigate the severity of Inuit/Indigenous experiences with the fallout from anti-sealing activism is undercut because there is a tendency in anti-sealing leaning scholarship and activist and media discourse to focus on the morality of seal hunting from a "is it cruel" perceptive or a focus on whether sealing provides adequate economic benefits for the Canadian economy (e.g. Sumner 1983; Butterworth and Richardson 2013). These approaches can result in ignoring the substantial cultural role of sealing in minority-dominated areas and the negative experiences had by non-Indigenous sealers at the hands of protesters and their supporters, which is also an important dimension to the sealing debate.

When local voices have tried to document and disseminate a counter-perceptive to academic assessments and activist narratives, they risk being targeted for bigotry, psychological and physical violence, such as Newfoundland filmmaker Anne Troake. Troake recounts that, among other things, she received death threats, ethnic slurs from prominent activists and a brick through her home window after releasing her 2005 documentary *My Ancestors Were Rogues and Murderers* in which she documented her family's struggle with anti-sealing activists and the fallout of decades of their campaigning (Interview with Anne Troake 2022 - see Burke 2023).[3]

While it might not be readily apparent why non-Indigenous experiences with anti-sealing campaigning undermine Inuit/Indigenous peoples, this book notes that there are close links between the two in the context of the public relations and broad cultural considerations given to sealing practices, economies and cultures by peoples outside of the cultural communities.[4] Many Inuit have been very open "that any opposition to the seal hunt, commercial or otherwise, harms Inuit by destroying the market for seal furs" (The Canadian Press 2014). Inuit pro-sealing campaigner Aaju Peter, for example, spoke out in 2017 in response to anti-commercial sealing videos by PETA. Peter argued that PETA "says there is no market. They crushed the market ... They made life very, very difficult" (CBC News 2017). At the time PETA released campaigning material against the North Atlantic commercial seal hunt in 2017, it also stated that it supports Inuit hunters. Peter, however, said work by organizations like PETA "creates a bad taste and a bad image" because their materials are misleading and promote a negative stereotype against the industry. Peter noted that "when PETA says baby seals are slaughtered ... They're not babies. Human beings have babies" (CBC News 2017), but the use of the "baby seal" trope continues to be very prevalent in anti-sealing narratives and framing.

The dehumanization of one class of sealers (commercial hunters, most especially non-Indigenous and non-observably Indigenous) as cruel savage slaughters while casting another class of hunters (Indigenous) as acceptable traditionalists makes it more difficult for Inuit/Indigenous sealing advocates to argue to external audiences like European policy makers why the European Union (EU) commercial seal product bans should end (for more information on Inuit attempts to overturn EU seal product bans see: Zilio 2013; Hennig 2015; also see European Commission 2016; 2019a, 2019b, for more on the

EU ban).[5] Therefore, this book posits that the normalization and devaluation of experiences of violence and trauma against certain cultural groups involved in the sealing debate, while framing others as deserving of some exception, has created a grey area for cultural violence to occur, and Newfoundlanders and Labradorians have fallen into this grey area.

Notes

1 In 2014 Greenpeace Canada apologized to Canadian Inuit and other Indigenous and coastal peoples for its anti-sealing conduct. In particular, Greenpeace Canada's 2014 apology expressed organizational awareness that its anti-sealing work was poorly executed to the detriment of others, with Greenpeace Canada particularly acknowledging the colonial approaches exhibited by anti-sealing protesters designed to impose their views and values on Indigenous (especially Inuit) and coastal peoples (Kerr 2014). Reflecting on Greenpeace's time campaigning against commercial sealing, Mads Flarup Christensen, executive director at Greenpeace Nordic acknowledged: "We got things wrong in the 70s around the sealing issue where I think we did not have sufficient know[ledge] or grounding in those areas and communities to really be able to, as city people and other countries, to go into areas and have a massive impact on local life" (Interview with Mads Flarup Christensen 2019 - see Burke 2020). Christensen's reflections and Greenpeace's 2014 apology for elements of its anti-sealing legacy point to some emerging awareness within the environmental movement that in the case of the anti-sealing protests, activist narratives and moral positioning of organizations and their opinions on seal hunting and the peoples involved in it may not be as congruent with the realities of what actually transpired, and continues to transpire, as those who support the anti-sealing cause might be led to believe.
2 Sealing also occurs to a lesser extent in parts of Nova Scotia, New Brunswick and Prince Edward Island.
3 The full interview with Anne Troake is published, open access, as part of the *Arctic* journal InfoNorth series (Burke 2023).
4 According to Jukka Nyyssönen, for example, in their work on Finnish Sámi and disputes over forest management in the 2000s, environmentalists sometimes have very romanticized views of Indigenous peoples and Indigenous Traditional Knowledge. The implication is that environmentalists sometimes have high expectations of Indigenous morality and knowledge with regard to their relationship with nature which can display "paternalism and intolerance". The idea, for example, that Indigenous peoples are inherently "natural conservationists", for example, can be "belittling" and limiting in terms of what people are encouraged to perceive as acceptable Indigenous uses of, and relationships with, non-human resources (Nyyssönen 2022, 2).
5 The EU ban is based on a moral objection (European Commission 2016; 2019a; 2019b). This ban is informed by anti-sealing advocacy and narratives from organizations like IFAW (IFAW n.d.) which also wants to be seen as supportive of Inuit/ Indigenous seal hunters (Wilkin 1998). Presently, the EU ban only makes allowances for seal product imports if they are (1) from Indigenous people and (2) only from subsistence hunting (European Commission 2016; 2019a; 2019b). This both ignores subsistence hunting practices and traditions by non-Indigenous peoples and limits Indigenous peoples from expanding locally based renewable sealing economies.

1 Stigmatization as a Tool of Cultural Violence

At the Heart of hardline anti-sealing activism is a strategy of stigmatization to both dissuade individuals, business and countries from association with anyone or anything connected to the practice of sealing and to justify and normalize behaviours, actions and attitudes against targets of anti-sealing activists and their supporters. To unpack the relationship between cultural violence, stigmatization and activism, the chapter first introduces the concept of culture. This sets the stage for the examination of the implications of breaking down the meanings and practices of a group through stigmatizing and alienating them, which can lead to the possible destruction of a group's cohesion by making group members fearful of, and threatened against, openly expressing or participating in the activities and beliefs that are central to the fabric of the group's identity.[1]

Culture and Cultural Violence

Broadly speaking, culture can be understood as "a system of meanings and practices that are transmitted and maintained over time by a group of people" and it "shapes individuals' understandings of the world and the self, enabling them to interact with others and the environment in ways considered appropriate by the group" (Kashima 2010, 164). However, culture is a fuzzy concept because "[m]eaning are a subjective part of culture that constitutes numerous beliefs, evaluations, expectations, ideas and various rules" which are shared and understood by a group of people (Kashima 2010, 164). Due to the fuzziness of culture, there are individuals and entities that argue that culture should be abandoned based on the belief that culture is "an obstacle for scientific progress" (Causadias 2020, 310). This idea that culture is a hindrance, and should potentially be eradicated because it is in the way of scientific progress is illustrated in a response to an op-ed piece about the impact of the anti-sealing movement on remote Indigenous and non-Indigenous communities in the Canadian Northeast written by this book's author.

An individual responding to a 2021 op-ed on the impact of the anti-sealing movement on sealing communities and families in coastal communities in Canada argued vehemently against sealing culture. The individual even went

DOI: 10.4324/9781003356158-2

so far as to state that Inuit are not "fully human" if they retain and practice sealing. The individual went on to state that sealing is "some stupid, irrelevant and moronic 'traditional' life style" because in their view:

> How many cancer scientists are never going to pick up a test tube or write a paper cos [*sic*] they are living impoverished and patheitc [*sic*] lives to provide seal fur to rich women to wear? How many rocket scientists [will] never see a rocket engine, how many virologists are up to their armpits in seal guts instead of working on a vaccine?

The individual's argument is that the world must stop seal hunting and other "noble savage" traditions because in their view to stop sealing is a net positive for the world because: "They [Inuit] deserve better than terrible homes in frigid and near uninhabitable environments, they should literally be moved and retrained for their own good and futures" (reader comments made in response to Burke 2021b).

According to Johan Galtung (1990, 291) cultural violence means that the "aspects of culture, the symbolic sphere of our existence – exemplified by religion and ideology, language and art, empirical science and formal science (logic, mathematics) – that can be used to justify or legitimize direct or structural violence". In the literature on the circumstances that result in forms of cultural violence, which at its most extreme can result in cultural genocide, common themes emerge in how situations unfold, and the mentality of individuals is expressed, that ultimately result in experiences of cultural violence. These themes include that: violence is typically unidirectional; violence tends to be inflicted against people identifiably different from the inflictors; perpetrators often believe that they are morally justified in their actions; for those experiencing the violence, there is a degree of immobility for them which means that those attacked cannot move elsewhere to continue their existence as a cohesive cultural group; and those perpetrating violence against a target group make an effort to assimilate their targets into their way of viewing the world (e.g. Belsky and Klagsbrun 2018; Campbell 2009; Kingston 2015; also see Burke 2021b, c).

The study of violence is about "the use of violence and the legitimatization of that use" (Galtung 1990, 291). The literature on cultural violence has evolved from the wider body of literature on cultural genocide, starting with Robert Lemkin and his struggle to get cultural genocide recognized as an issue beyond the overarching term (physical) genocide in the post-Second World War development of human rights laws (e.g. Novic 2016; Payam 2016; Berster 2015; Kingston 2015). Cultural genocide is "the destruction of those structures and practices that allow the group to continue as a group" (Truth and Reconciliation Report 2015). Since Lemkin's introduction, recognition of cultural genocide as a concept and the factors that lead to it have grown. As recognition of cultural genocide has grown the term has evolved to reflect a gradual shift in thinking from a focus on tangible cultural heritage, such as monuments and art, toward the inclusion of intangible elements of culture such as languages and traditional practices (e.g. Belsky and Klagsbrun 2018; Mullen 2020).

There is an emerging body of literature dedicated to case studies of cultural genocide and cultural violence that explore the most extreme forms of cultural violence that escalate to cultural genocide in recent memory. The most prominent examples in the literature are the experiences of Indigenous peoples whose children were forced into residential schools run by states and religious organizations in many areas of Canada and Australia resulting in thousands of deaths and attempts at assimilate children through the destruction of Indigenous languages and the prevention of the passing on of Indigenous Traditional Knowledge (e.g. Kingston 2015; Mahoney 2019; Paquette 2020; van Krieken 1999). There is also the example of the ethnic cleansing in the former Yugoslavia which encapsulated cultural violence leading to cultural and physical genocide (e.g. Novic 2016; Mullen 2020; Berster 2015). Both of the above examples that are frequently associated with cultural genocide and acts of cultural violence in current literature focus on the state and state-supported actors as the central perpetrator(s) of violence. Traditional political actors such as states and organized religions continue to dominate the case study explorations of cultural genocide and cultural violence. This book posits that more contemporary actors like environmental and animal rights organizations can also act in ways which inflict and encourage cultural violence and contribute to circumstances that can result in cultural violence being inflicted by third parties persuaded by their narratives, arguments and worldviews.

While this book does not argue that the anti-sealing experiences of fishers/sealers, their families and communities in Newfoundland and Labrador, or other rural and coastal non-Indigenous sealing societies in northeastern Canada, reach the threshold of cultural genocide yet, it does argue that acts of cultural violence have been, and continue to be, experienced as a result of anti-sealing protesters and the organizations leading the cause. There appears to be an underpinning desire by some protesters to suppress the province's cultural and economic sealing practices that are embedded in the traditional Newfoundland and Labrador society, especially those associated with non-Indigenous peoples. Furthermore, the cultural violence being experienced by Newfoundland and Labrador sealers, their families and communities has been normalized and ignored by many academics, mainstream media and activists. The normalization and ignoring of cultural violence has occurred through the repetition of activist narratives and actions and the wilful blindness of media outlets, politicians and authority figures to the harms being inflicted and experienced by rural and coastal communities and their peoples.

According to Johan Galtung,

To some, this [siege/blockade (classical term) and sanctions (modern term)] is "non-violence", since direct and immediate killing is avoided. To the victims, however, it may mean slow but intentional killing through malnutrition and lack of medical attention, hitting the weakest first, the children, the elderly, the poor, the women. By making the causal chain longer the actor avoids having to face the violence directly ... meaning the loss of freedom and identity instead of loss of life and limbs. (1990, 293)

As this book illustrates, cultural violence is insidious because it "makes direct and structural violence look, even feel, right – or at least not wrong" (Galtung, 1990, 291). Anti-sealing protesters have illustrated, as this book will show, that they are skilled at presenting direct and structural forms of violence against rural and coastal sealers, their families and communities as a net positive for the world (e.g. Felsberg, 1985; IFAW, n.d.).[2]

Stigmatization as a Tool of Cultural Violence

The process of stigmatization is a key way in which environmental and animal rights organizations have approached issues and topics that they seek to shame and devalue to justify their position against an "other" and convince people to support their cause and methods of pursuing it. The stigmatization process is central in a lot of activism because at the heart of activism is a competition for moral legitimacy.

Moral legitimacy is socially constructed by giving and considering the reasons for justifying certain actions, practices, or institutions ... audiences can assess an organization's moral legitimacy by evaluating ... outputs and consequences (doing the rights things), techniques and procedures (doing things rights), categories and structures (the right organisation for the job), and leaders and representatives (the right person in charge of the tasks).

(Liu et al. 2014, 635)

Moral legitimacy is the primary form of legitimacy that activist organizations claim to possess as they present themselves as operating on behalf of the common good (Baur and Palazzo 2011, 584; Marberg et al. 2016, 2737–8).

The repercussions of a lack of perceived moral legitimacy can hinder an actor, such as an environmental or animal rights organization, because they are tied to the idea that they help to "point out problems in society and give a voice to the marginalized, and this 'moral voice' is what strengthens their legitimacy" (Puljek-Shank 2019, 7). Therefore in the pursuit of a cause, environmental activist organizations must find ways to establish and maintain a perception of moral legitimacy for their attitudes, actions and the outcomes of their lobbying and advocacy amongst their core supporters and desired audiences for their messaging because moral legitimacy is "the most meaningful type for judging the legitimacy of NGOs" (Baur & Palazzo 2011, 584).

Though stigma can have both negative and positive forms (Page 1984), typically stigma and stigmatization are viewed as having a negative connotation. Pescosolido and Martin (2015, 91) define stigma as "the mark, the condition, or status that is subject to devaluation" whereas stigmatization is "the social process by which the mark [of stigma] affects the lives of all those touched by it" (Page 1984, 16). Stigma is often associated with negative connotations and results when actors label others in a derogatory way to brand them as "deviant and undesirable" (Connor 2014). The attribution of a stigma can also be used to convince audiences that actors, places, things or issues "possess (or are believed to possess) some attribute, or characteristic, that conveys a social identity that is devalued in a particular social context" (Crocker, Major and Steele 1998, 505, as quoted in Blodorn & Major 2016).

Thornicroft et al. (2007, 192) argue that "stigma refers to problems of knowledge (ignorance), attitudes (prejudice) and behaviour (discrimination)" and "is a mark or sign of disgrace usually eliciting negative attitudes to its bearer". Stigma can lead to negative discrimination and "is sometimes but not always related to a lack of knowledge about the condition that led to stigmatization" (Thornicroft et al. 2007, 192). Though there are variations in the definitions of stigma in academic literature (Link and Phelan 2001, 364–5), Thornicroft et al.'s (2007) definition of stigma in the context of people dealing with mental health challenges encapsulates key notions of stigma that are important to remember when discussing the concept and its implications in the context of this book: stigma typically has a negative connotation; there are risks associated with the discrimination for those who become stigmatized; and stigma often results from a stigmatizer's lack of knowledge.

Another important dimension of stigma to consider when discussing both stigma and its ties to cultural violence is that behind the attribution of stigma are the motives of a stigmatizer. According to Link and Phelan (2014, 25) "whether it is to keep people down, in, or away ... we might expect people to use power to achieve the ends they desire ... stigma is frequently the power mechanism of choice". For instance, Phelan et al. (2008) identify three broad ends that people can achieve through stigma.

In the first, exploitation and domination or "keeping people down," wealth, power, and high social status can be attained when one group dominates or exploits another ... In the second, enforcement of social norms or "keeping people in" ... Stigma imparts a stiff cost that can both keep the norm violator in and serve as a reminder to others that they should remain in as well ... In the third, avoidance of disease or "keeping people away" ... The evolutionary advantage of avoiding disease might have led to a more general distaste for deviations from any local standard for the way humans are supposed to look or carry themselves leading to a strong desire to stay away from people who deviate with respect to a broad band of physical or behavioral characteristics.

(Phelan et al. 2008 as discussed in Link and

Phelan 2014, 24–5)

Link and Phelan argue that "[w]hen people have an interest in keeping other people down, in or away, stigma is a resource that allows them to obtain [the] ends they desire". Link and Phelan refer to this resource as "stigma power" which they discuss as "instances in which stigma processes achieve the aims of stigmatizers with respect to the exploitation, management, control or exclusion of others" (Link and Phelan 2014, 24).

Link and Phelan draw upon the work of Bourdieu and symbolic power to make their case about the connections between stigma and power. They point out that "[f]or Bourdieu (1987) symbolic power is the capacity to impose on others a legitimatized vision of the social world and the cleavages within that world" (Bourdieu 1987 as paraphrased in Link and Phelan 2014, 25).

Indeed Bourdieu argues that:

> What is at stake in symbolic struggles is the imposition of the legitimate vision of the social world and of its divisions, that is to say, symbolic power ... the power to impose and to inculcate [teach] principles of construction of reality, and particularly to preserve or transform established principles of union and separation, of association and disassociation already at work in the social world such as current classifications in matters of gender, age, ethnicity, region or nation, that is, essentially, power over words used to describe groups or the institutions which represent them.
>
> (Bourdieu 1987, 13–14)

The struggle for the imposition of a legitimate social world vision is important to recognize to better understand stigma and the interconnectedness of the concept with instances of cultural violence. This is because "cultural distinctions of value and worth are critically important mechanisms through which power is exercised" and stigma is a form of symbolic power because "stigma represents a statement about value and worth made by stigmatizers about those they stigmatize" (Link and Phelan 2014, 25).

Since the 1980s, non-governmental organization (NGO) advocacy has risen, as has the number of NGOs (Collingwood 2006, 440; also see Dhanani and Connolly 2015) with growing involvement in politics and policy-making (Vedder 2007, 1; also see Jenkins 2012, 460). Advocacy is the effort to change institutions, actors and policy and is "based upon policy analysis, research, and the channelling of information" (Hudson 2001, 333). According to Betsill and Corell (2007, 2), "[d]espite mounting evidence that NGOs make a difference in global environmental politics, the question of under what conditions NGOs matter generally remains unanswered". One big issue at the centre of discussions about NGO influence focuses on legitimacy with questions such as: "Who do they represent?" (Hudson 2001, 331; also see Ossewaarde et al. 2008). Awareness about the growing power and impact of activists is on the rise, and as a result, debate over non-governmental organization conduct and the legitimacy of undemocratically elected entities to claim to represent large segments of society and have a significant impact on policy and the lives of vulnerable peoples are being questioned. Questions about non-governmental organizations' legitimacy arise in part because these political actors operate from the basis of moral preferences (Baron 2001) and they are not directly accountable to the public despite impacting the daily lives of people and "wield[ing] power in ways similar to governments" (Vedder 2007, 7). NGOs use threats and their private potential to harm actors to push for change. The potential to harm can be achieved through activities such as boycotts, naming and shaming, and cyber-activism (Daubanes and Rochet 2016, 1). With such power to impact peoples' lives, it is therefore incumbent upon us to question how NGOs work and achieve their outcomes and the role that strategies like stigmatization and the normalization of forms of violence play in their effort to shape society's moral preferences.

Notes

1 In this book sometimes you will see the words "non-violent", "nonviolent", "non-violence" and "nonviolence", depending on quotes and sources referenced. This is something to note as according to Baldoli and Radaelu (2019, 1166) the hyphen is significant in the nonviolence literature (see Sharp 2005) as the hyphen is often viewed as a demarcation of mindset toward the concept of nonviolence. Baldoli and Radaelu observe that those that tend toward the use of the hyphen are often associated with viewing nonviolence as merely the absence of violence. The specialized literature on nonviolence, however, often using the spelling "nonviolence" rather than "non-violence" because "nonviolence" has positive properties beyond the refusal to not use violence (Baldoli and Radaelu 2019, 1166; Sharp 2005).

2 IFAW states on its website that in response to the Government of Canada raising seal hunt quotas in the 1990s, the organization "knew we needed to do more than just raise awareness. So we partnered with European politicians to implement a European ban on all seal products. And we worked to defend this ban when it was challenged by Canada and Norway at the World Trade Organization. Once that ban was in place, the number of Canadian sealers dropped by 90 percent" (IFAW, n.d.). Unacknowledged in IFAWs declaration, for example, is that EU ban is based on "moral concerns regarding seal welfare" rather than scientific evidence, for example, about the survival of the species (World Trade Organization, 2014) and the IFAW statement does not acknowledge that Canadian Inuit, as represented by the Inuit Tapiriit Kanatami, are against the EU ban that IFAW pushed for and have denounced the WTO ruling (Nunatsiaq News, 2013; World Trade Organisation, 2014). Additionally the idea is presented by IFAW that a 90 percent loss of sealers in Canada is inherently good. IFAW does not acknowledge or give value to the cultural, economic and societal repercussions that a rapid 90 percent loss of active sealers would have on the cohesion of cultural groups with strong ties to sealing, its members and community structures.

2 An Overview

Sealing and the Anti-Sealing Movement in the Canadian North Atlantic and Arctic

In the Canadian North and Northeast, sealing is an ancient practice that Indigenous and non-Indigenous peoples and communities have participated in for generations. This chapter provides a brief overview of subsistence and commercial sealing in the Canadian context and an introduction to the rise of the anti-sealing movement. It presents some of the big factors that influenced the evolution of the anti-sealing movement, such as the debate over the definition of cruelty, and the power of optics and setting the narrative. The chapter explores the importance of the anti-sealing movement's early success in defining global ideas about what is sealing and who are sealers and the problems that rural and coastal peoples in Newfoundland and Labrador face as a result of their substantial disadvantages when trying to be heard, understood and represented in the national and international debate about their cultural and economic practices and traditional way of life.

Sealing Cultural Heritage in Newfoundland and Labrador: A Brief Introduction

> Sealing was a key, an integral, part of the settlement and evolution of people in coastal Newfoundland and Labrador, the Magdalen Islands, the Quebec North Shore, Nunavut and the Northwest Territories. There is an old saying in Newfoundland which sums up the role of sealing in most coastal communities: king cod and queen seal. Nature in these areas is harsh and in order to survive one needs success in a variety of employments to make a living and sealing was one of them.
> (Interview with James Winter 2021 - see Burke 2022a)

According to James Winter, a former Canadian Broadcasting Corporation (CBC) journalist and founding president of the Canadian Sealers Association, sealing is deeply rooted in Newfoundland and Labrador's economic and cultural history, but its role has been misrepresented by activists to the point that many people around the world do not know the facts behind the "why" of sealing practices in isolated and rural coastal communities in the Canadian

DOI: 10.4324/9781003356158-3

Arctic and Northeast Coast and are quick to dismiss sealing as unnecessary and wrong.

> People sealed for generations because of the "hungry month of March" that plagued their lives. The cash in hand gave some independence from the "truck system" that dominated village life. The truck system is an economic system wherein one is tied to a village merchant who carries credit and pays in script. He [the merchant] sets the price of goods and the price you receive for your products and labour. This system dominated life in the sealing communities for hundreds of years. Sealing not only helped people through the harsh times of the late winter and early spring, but because of the cash in hand a limited sense of independence was created. It also created an emotional attachment to the actions of the men who risked their lives for their families and their community. Out of sealing sprang the songs, the stories, the literature, and the self-identification that celebrated the people, the successes, the disasters, and the deaths – of which there were many – that were at the core of sealing and of village life: the culture of the society.
> (Interview with James Winter 2021 - see Burke 2022a)

The connection between working-class people and the seal hunt arose from the traditional seasonal fishing cycle in Newfoundland and Labrador and is cemented in the identity and cultural heritage of long-standing multigenerational families and communities in Newfoundland and Labrador (see Sanger 1998).

The long-standing practice of seal hunting in Newfoundland and Labrador society developed a "culture, and working-class solidarity among the sealing community" (Harter 2004, 93) and led to a formation of a class of individuals known as "sealers" notably different "from the more typical development of waged workers in Canada" (Harter 2004, 94). But communicating about the cultural importance of sealing can be challenging for audiences not from, and actively part of, a culture because "the culturally meaningful aspect of sealing is rarely discussed except among insiders, using an *insider's* code" which means that for an outsider it can be "confusing and difficult if not impossible" to appreciate the "experiential, evaluative meaning" of the culture for the in-group members (Wright 1981, 62; also see Burke 2022b for reflections on the author's experience as an "in-group" member). This challenge in communicating the cultural meaning and importance to non-group members is important to appreciate in this context because what has largely been underplayed and undervalued by protesters in the sealing debate is how deeply embedded seal hunting is in the legacy of survival, family, working-class rights and perseverance associated with generations of fishing communities and their families in Newfoundland and Labrador. As Guy Wright observed in his study on the cultural and economic reasons for participation in the Newfoundland and Labrador seal hunt:

> The risk and hardship involved in the seal hunt have loaded it with cultural meaning. The hunt echoes the history of a poor colony whose citizens were exploited by a ruling elite and who had to survive in a marginal environment. It has become a metaphor for all that is strong and stoic in Newfoundland's [and Labrador's] collective ethos.
>
> (Wright 1981, 61)

The working-class legacy of coastal communities and the struggle for workers' rights and the profound costs many families paid to survive in the harsh economic and climatic conditions of the Northwest Atlantic is a central element of Newfoundland and Labrador's history. The history of workers' rights and working-class survival is memorialized and lamented in the province through events like the 1914 SS *Newfoundland* sealing disaster. As part of the March 1914 seal hunt, 132 sealers from the SS *Newfoundland* became stranded on the ice sheets of the North Atlantic for two days and nights during a blizzard resulting in many of the men freezing to death. In the end only 55 men survived (Higgins 2013). Images are seared in the collective memory of Newfoundland and Labrador society of the horror stories that emerged from "The Front" after the disaster of men and their young sons froze to death, huddled together on one last desperate family embrace, trying unsuccessfully stay warm and survive the blizzard (Brown and Horwood 1972).

The same year, 1914, saw the sinking of the SS *Southern Cross* on its return from the seal hunt. Details of what happened to the SS *Southern Cross* are limited because it sunk "[w]ithout any surviving witnesses, wireless communication, or ship logs"; all 174 men went down with the vessel. In total the "SS *Southern Cross* and SS *Newfoundland* suffered a combined loss of 251 men, leaving hardly any person or community unaffected by the events" (Dawson 2014). The disasters have stood the test of time in Newfoundland and Labrador's historical memory because it is tied to issues of class that dominated the early 20th century in the country, now a Canadian province. Issues of merchant greed resulting in ship captains being pressured to push impoverished sealers to take more and more risks to get pelts if they wanted to be paid and a lack of investment by companies in safety equipment for vessels (e.g. radios for ship to ship and ice to ship communication) and a lack of care about workers (e.g. lack of food, work clothing for the weather conditions) were major debates in Newfoundland and Labrador at that time. Sealing was at the centre of many of the tragic instances of elite greed trumping peoples' welfare (Brown and Horwood 1972; also see Cadigan 2013).[1]

When the protests against rural and coastal sealing arose in the decades after the 1914 disaster, the protests and their strategies and tactics were not, and are not, simply experienced and viewed as a protest against seal hunting in the Newfoundland and Labrador context; they are experienced as a deliberate and malicious devaluation and dismissal by predominately urban-based cultural outsiders against centuries of rural and coastal traditions, survival and sacrifice by working-class families. The enduring cultural connection to sealing and the collective traumatic experiences associated with fishing tragedies and subsequent anti-sealing protests help to explain why sealing and sealers are strongly supported in the province to this day despite the decades of campaigning intended to vilify the practice of seal hunting. Monica Engel, Jerry Vaske and Alistair Bath (2021), for example, conducted a survey on local perceptions about the seal hunt in Newfoundland and Labrador that was distributed to 38 rural and 2 urban communities (40 communities total), resulting in 773 coastal residents completing the questionnaire (52 percent men and 48 percent women) with the respondents being based in both rural (53 percent) and urban (47 percent) locations.

According to Engel et al. (2021, 4) their questionnaire reveals that in Newfoundland and Labrador the use of "seals for commercial and subsistence purposes was [viewed as] acceptable among respondents, with no significant difference between urban and rural respondents. Only 8% of the respondents did not accept using seals". Furthermore 71 percent of respondents either agreed or strongly agreed that seals are an important part of the Newfoundland and Labrador economy and 77 percent held positive attitudes toward seals (16 percent were neutral) with a large portion of respondents also expressing concern about the role of seals in the decline of the cod population (Ibid).[2] Additionally Engel et al. (2021) acknowledge that their questionnaire results reveal that "urban residents held stronger ecological and intrinsic [seal value orientations] SVOs, [while] rural residents held stronger cultural and instrumental SVOs" (2021, 4) and stress that seals are valued for reasons beyond nutritional and economic benefits with local people recognizing their instrumental and cultural importance (2021, 7).[3]

Subsistence and Commercial Sealing: A Brief Introduction

While commercial sealing based from large ships is the prominent image of seal hunting that many people have, with dozens of men pouring on the ice pans covered in harp seals and their pups, this is an incomplete and out-of-date picture that fails to capture the complexity and evolution of seal hunting as a practice and how it is conducted today. Generally speaking, there are two ways of seal hunting in the Canadian Arctic and Northeast – from land and from a ship/vessel; landmens venture onto coastal ice and hunt from the shoreline or small boats and fishers go offshore hunting from longliners and large vessels[4] on the ice pans that flow down the Northwest Atlantic seasonally from the high Canadian and Greenlandic Arctic around March–May (Murphy 1916; Fisheries and Oceans Canada 1979). Seal hunting has occurred in the area of present-day Canada for generations, and there are two broad, but sometimes overlapping, categories under which it occurs: subsistence and commercial.

Subsistence hunting has a longer history than commercial hunting with Indigenous and later non-Indigenous hunters using seals for generations for their survival in the harsh northern and northeastern climates (Fisheries and Oceans Canada 1979).[5] Non-Indigenous coastal peoples in the Canadian Northeast, especially in coastal communities in Newfoundland and Labrador, the Quebec North Shore and the Magdalen Islands, have been subsistence hunting seals for hundreds of years, while Indigenous peoples have been hunting for much longer. The Indigenous people most readily associated with seal hunting are Inuit whose homelands stench across the Canadian Arctic (Inuit Nunangat[6]) (e.g. Fisheries and Oceans Canada 2011; Interim Report to the Minister of Environment from the Committee on Seals and Sealing 1972, 4).[7] However, in Newfoundland and Labrador, for example, in addition to Inuit, other Indigenous peoples such as the Innu in Labrador (Department of Fisheries and Oceans 1979)[8] and the Mi'kmaq on the Island of Newfoundland also traditionally hunt and use seals (e.g. Benoit First Nation 2016; Qalipu First Nation 2020). The subsistence hunting of seals is less controversial as it is hunting primarily for personal use and on a comparatively smaller scale to commercial hunting. Indigenous subsistence hunting, with a focus on Inuit in particular, is implicitly communicated in recent years by environmental organizations like Greenpeace and PETA, and by the EU, as the tolerable form of sealing (e.g. Kerr 2014; Burgwald 2016; PETA n.d.; European Commission 2016; 2019a, 2019b).

The commercial seal hunt, however, is the primary target of anti-sealing campaigners (e.g. IFAW 2020; Patey 1990). Originally in the 1960s–1980s the desired outcomes of anti-sealing campaigners ranged from calls for improvement to harp seal stock management and more hunting oversight to outright calls to end all commercial sealing (Phelps Bondaroff and Burke 2014; Patey 1990). The moderate calls for improvements to seal stock management and improve hunting safety and oversight were addressed relatively early in the protests (Phelps Bondaroff and Burke 2014). Currently anti-sealing advocacy is less prominent and largely focused on calls to outright end commercial sealing.

Historically the majority of the commercial seal hunt based in North America in the Northwest Atlantic occurred off the coast of Newfoundland and Labrador in an area known as "The Front". The hunting was conducted from big ships that could carry dozens or more sealers. Sealing vessels came from Newfoundland and Labrador, as well as other parts of Canada (mainly Quebec with some sealing based out of Nova Scotia, Prince Edward Island and New Brunswick) and from Europe, such as from Norway and Greenland, and hundreds of thousands of seals were hunted annually. While this picture of seal hunting continues to dominate the public imagination, it is an image of sealing from a by-gone era.

It is true, for example, that in 1840, 600,000 seal pelts, mainly harp seals, were landed in Newfoundland and Labrador (Murphy 1916). This number of seal pelts does not include any pelts lost, miscounted, or landed in other neighbouring regions that sent ships to hunt from the same herd such as Canada (Newfoundland and Labrador did not join Canada until 1949 – Cochrane and Parsons 1949) or from Greenland (Fisheries and Oceans Canada 1979).[9] Almost 170 years later in 2009, however, only 91,000 seals were landed in all of Canada which Newfoundland and Labrador is now a part of, including seal species other than harp seals (the primary commercial seal hunted in Canada).[10] By 2010 the number dipped further to 67,000 landed pelts with the decreasing number caused by factors such as sea ice conditions, market value of pelts and export market access limitations (Fisheries and Oceans Canada 2011).

The decrease in seal hunting in Canada has also occurred as a result of conservation efforts (e.g. Farquhar 2020; Hawkins and Silver 2017; Lafrance 2017)[11] coupled with changes in Canada's offshore jurisdiction (e.g. Dale and Mills 1979; Stanford 1979) which enable the Government of Canada to more effectively monitor and control legal access to areas where seal hunting occurs.[12] However, the primary reason why seal hunting has decreased so drastically is because of limited access to international marketplaces for Canadian sealing products and the stigmatization of seal products.

International product import bans were instigated after pressure from anti-sealing protesters and their potent narratives and media campaigns resulted in the widespread stigmatization of seal products, the sealing industry and anybody associated with either. In 1972, for example, the United States banned seal product imports, though the United States was only a small market for seal products so the ban had limited effect on its own. However, in 1983 the European Economic Community followed the United States with a ban on whitecoat harp seal furs, which was the most economically lucrative export from Canada (Dauvergne and Neville 2011). The European Union, which succeeded the European Economic Community, followed up its targeted ban in 2009, with an outright ban on all seal product imports (European Commission 2019b).[13] While this is not an inclusive list of all bans on Canadian seal products either from state/pan state marketplaces or by individual businesses, such as the Tesco grocery store chain in the United Kingdom (Hawkins and Silver 2017), it does illustrate that the campaigns to devalue sealing as a practice, and seal products as its output, have been highly successful, especially with the European audiences. The European bans on seal products effectively crippled the economic viability of much of the Canadian sealing export market because for centuries Europe was the primary marketplace for the products.

Emergence of the Anti-Sealing Movement

The anti-sealing movement formally started in 1969.[14] It was a movement made up of environmental and animal rights activists and protestors, with support for media outlets, celebrities and politicians. It focused on emotional images, messages and advocacy to challenge the legitimacy of seal hunting (Phelps Bondaroff and Burke 2014). A major point of contention wedged between the emotion-versus-science push and pull of the campaigning and counter-campaigning is whether the seal hunt was cruel. The Interim Committee on Seals and Sealing (1972, 4) ruled that:

> There is no evidence ... to suggest that [a sealer] is any less humane than any other human being. In fact, the Committee has received no evidence that there is any degree of intentional cruelty involved in sealing and that, to the contrary, every indication is that the sealers are aware of their obligation to kill the seals humanely, and are making a very definite attempt to do just that.

IFAW, for example, disagrees with the view that sealing is not intentionally cruel.

IFAW has long been the leading organization in the loose coalition of actors that make up the anti-sealing movement, and it defines cruelty as "[b]ehavior which causes physical or mental harm to another individual [animals], whether intentional or not" (IFAW 2020). As such IFAW position's is that "commercial sealing should be prohibited as they are inherently cruel, unnecessary, and can pose a serious threat to the survival of these species" (IFAW 2020).[15] Ironically this same lens of viewing cruelty as any behaviour that causes physical or mental harm is not used by IFAW to reflect on the legacy of the anti-sealing movement itself.

Realistically sealing is an easy target for environmental and animal rights campaigners. Sealing predominantly occurs in rural, isolated locations by working-class individuals (e.g. Harter 2004; Burke 2021c; Phelps Bondaroff and Burke 2014). It is a messy, dangerous activity that operates out in the open on floating sea ice. It is impossible to hide what is happening during seal hunting compared to commercial slaughterhouses for the cattle and pork industries, for example.

While sealing has helped to sustain the cultures, societies and economies of thousands of working-class rural and coastal communities and peoples for generations, it is a public relations nightmare and the industry and cultures associated with sealing practices and traditions are poorly understood. James Winter acknowledged that:

> The fact that sealing takes place in far-away communities and the many people involved are mostly descendants of European immigrants made sealers an easy target. Anti-sealing corporations attempted to sell the idea that they were not against "Indigenous" non-commercial sealing. This politically correct meaningless distinction failed as the Indigenous market collapsed despite the fact they did not hunt "whitecoats". The

impact on Indigenous communities was huge as most had fewer options than other sealers to replace the lost activity and income.

(Interview with James Winter 2021 - see Burke 2022a)[16]

The sealing industry is plagued with the stark portrayals of hot, red blood splattered on frozen white ever-moving ice pans; a sight that has created some of the most powerful mental, photographic and film imagery of the 20th century.

Therefore, images of dead seals and blood-soaked ice help to create a powerful myth which transcended attempts to get public audiences to see beyond them.

[W]hat remains with the individual affected by this propaganda is a perfectly irrational picture, a purely emotional feeling, a myth. The fact is the data, the reasoning – all are forgotten, and only the impression remains. And this is indeed what the propagandist ultimately seeks, for the individual will never begin to act on the basis of facts or engage in purely rational behavior. What makes him act is the emotional pressure, the vision of a future, the myth. The problem is to create an irrational response on the basis of rational and factual elements.

(Ellul 1965, 86–87 as quoted in Lowe 2008, 72)

Regardless of what anyone may think about what environmental or animal rights organizations say or have said, portrayed or did during their respective anti-sealing campaigns, particularly IFAW, PETA and Greenpeace (and later Sea Shepherd),[17] their use of emotional imagery through photography, filmography and rhetoric set the international tone against rural peoples. Indeed, according to Ian Urbina (2019) Greenpeace and Sea Shepherd have a history of believing "that the ends justified the means. They were willing to operate outside the law".

As the anti-sealing narratives surrounding the seal hunt emerged in the 1960s–1980s,[18] so too did the reality for locals that the more they tried to defend themselves, the more they seemed to lose the argument (e.g. Felsberg 1985; Patey 1990). According to Jacques Ellul and his research on propaganda, the irony is that the more information/data people get about something, the more they lean toward simplified explanations of the subject:

[M]uch of the information disseminated nowadays – research findings, facts, statistics, explanations, analyses – *eliminate* personal judgment and the capacity to form one's own opinion even more surely than the most extravagant propaganda. This claim may seem shocking; but it is a

> fact that excessive data do not enlighten the reader or the listener; they
> drown him ... the more facts supplied, the more simplistic the image.
>
> (Ellul 1965, 87)

Locals tried to provide counter information. For example, in St. Anthony, Newfoundland, a small northern coastal community where many sealers were based and where protestors spent a lot of time attacking local people and practices on the ground, a local group called the St. Anthony Citizens' Committee formed to try and stop the anti-sealing forces from destroying their way of life (Patey 1990, 22). As the protests became more intense, some government actors tried to provide an outlet to partially help locals be heard in the debate. For example, a brief for Canada's *Royal Commission on Seals and Sealing Industry in Canada* (1985) provided an avenue for local peoples to express their concerns and hurt at the economic, cultural and societal impact of the protests, protestors, media coverage, government responses and market closures and decrease product demand due to stigmatization of fur.[19]

While locals struggled at the height of the anti-sealing movement to communicate about the value and importance of sealing to their communities, economies and cultures, individual environmental and animal rights organizations also faced the challenge of distinguishing themselves as the agenda of what various actors in the anti-sealing movement were trying to accomplish became blurred and more hardline (e.g. Felsberg 1985; Royal Commission on Seals and Sealing Industry in Canada 1985). According to Phelps Bondaroff and Burke (2014, 169)

> the anti-sealing movement had two primary goals. While some organizations, including the Audubon Society, the WWF, and the Canadian Wildlife Federation, focused on the harp seal's long-term survival, others, especially animal welfare organizations such as the RSPCA and HSC, placed emphasis on the way the hunt was conducted.[20]

By the mid- to late 1970s, more hardline views against sealing were promoted by organizations like IFAW and Greenpeace. Their narratives began to dominate news coverage and public perception of the protests with their image events and slick PR campaigns (Patey 1990; Harter 2004). IFAW, in particular, focused on documenting and photographing "alleged atrocities of the hunt and disseminat[ing] powerful graphic images globally" (Phelps Bondaroff and Burke 2014, 170). It undertook a campaign characterized by "sociological warfare" which according to Brian Lowe "is a conflict that is intended to alter one or more aspects of the public moral imagination regarding at least one issue, practice, or phenomena" (Lowe 2008, 70).

By 1983 when the European Economic Community (EEC) ban on whitecoat harp seal products was implemented (European Commission 2019a), many organizations that were involved in raising various issues with sealing management, practices and hunting had achieved their objectives (Phelps Bondaroff and Burke 2014). Others, however, became aware that the narratives and information from organizations in the movement had caused unintended consequences (Woods 1986; Phelps Bondaroff and Burke 2014; Kerr 2014) and questions about activism legitimacy began to creep more prominently into the sealing debate (e.g. for more on the broader issue activism legitimacy see Hudson 2001).

Greenpeace is the best example of an organization that was hardline against sealing, had a leading role in the anti-sealing movement in the 1970s and played a foundational role in stigmatizing sealing and sealers to global audiences (Burke 2020), but has since come to regret and reject aspects of its involvement in the anti-sealing cause (Kerr 2014). By the late 1980s, Greenpeace began to publicly acknowledge some of the damage of their work and that of the anti-sealing movement as a whole on Inuit and other Indigenous peoples (Woods 1986). While Greenpeace remains opposed to commercial sealing (Burgwald 2016), it is trying to be more nuanced about its stance on subsistence and Indigenous hunting and has withdrawn from actively campaigning against sealing. It has also publicly apologized for some elements of its conduct during the protests which undermined the rights and economic structures of Inuit, Indigenous and coastal peoples (Kerr 2014), though the apology predominately focused on the Inuit dimension of its harmful legacy (Burke 2021c).

While the anti-sealing cause continues to the present day, it does not garner as much publicity and media spotlight as it did in the 1970s–1980s. Organizations like IFAW and PETA continue to position themselves against commercial sealing and only state marginal support sealing if conducted by Inuit/Indigenous for "subsistence" purposes. However, as the next chapter elaborates, untangling subsistence and commercial sealing is not as straightforward conceptually and culturally as environmental and animal rights organizations make it appear. As a result, proclamations of support for subsistence versus commercial sealing and the killing of seals for traditional purposes by one ethnic group or class of peoples versus another can be highly divisive and problematic, especially for organizations that purport to believe that the killing of animals is inherently cruel.

Notes

1 The 1914 sealing disaster was instrumental in creating support for the Fishermen's Protective Union (FPU), led by William Coaker, who was enraged by the neglect and abuse of the working-class people of output communities by the merchant class and industrial interests (Cadigan 2013).

2 Engel et al. note that there is "a strong belief that seals were causing the decline of Atlantic cod, and the federal government was not managing the situation appropriately. Evidence shows that predation by grey seals may account for up to 50% of natural cod mortality in the southern Gulf of St. Lawrence, but with an unclear

effect on the low recovery of cod populations in the area" (2021, 6). The authors also note that their questionnaire reveals that "[c]oastal residents were asked to what extent they trusted the federal government in managing the ocean in the province. About 22% did not trust the government at all, 43% trusted just a little, 32% said they trusted the federal government about half of the time, and 3% always trusted the government for managing the ocean. Rural residents expressed significantly less trust in the federal government than urban respondents" (Ibid).

3 Engel et al. argue that the foundation of hierarchical relationships are values and value orientations, and they help predict "variability in attitudes and behaviours" with SVOs "classified as intrinsic and instrumental, where seals are valued beyond their economic and nutritional benefits" with the analysis of SVOs including cultural and ecological value orientations (2021, 2).

4 According to a former Department of Fisheries and Oceans Canada officer who worked in Newfoundland and Labrador on issues such as the management and monitoring of the seal hunt, seal hunting by long vessels is discontinued in Canada. Longliners are still used and are approximately 20 feet in length.

5 Sealing is a common practice throughout the Canadian North. There is no fixed definition of the North in Canada, but eminent scholars in the field acknowledge that the general perception of where is the Canadian North is not static and has gradually receded further North (Elliot-Meisel 1998; Grant, 1989), with the North being made up of the Arctic and the sub-Arctic (Burke 2018). For the purposes of this book the Canadian North is defined to include much of the upper portions of the Canadian mainland provinces (excluding Nova Scotia, Prince Edward Island and New Brunswick) and the whole of Newfoundland and Labrador. This definition is meant to acknowledge of areas throughout Canada which have traditionally been part of the North and in which people there continue to identify as being northerners with northern historical, cultural, societal and economic roots (Stone, 1954). Areas such as the Island of Newfoundland presently have a more contested placement within 21st century definitions of the North as defined by academics and central Canadian government bodies, the overwhelming majority of which are not based in Newfoundland, nor have historical ties to the province whose history is somewhat disconnected from Canada since it only joined Canada in 1949 (Cochrane and Parsons 1949). However, the Island of Newfoundland has long historical, cultural, societal and economic roots connected to its northern (sub-Arctic) heritage (with Labrador being the historical and geographic Arctic as the upper portion of the province) which persists in the daily lives of people on the island particularly in many non-urban areas into present times (Burke 2021a).

6 According to the Inuit Tapiriit Kanatami "Inuit Nunangat is a distinct geographic, political and cultural region that includes the Inuvialuit Settlement Region (Northwest Territories), Nunavut, Nunavik (Northern Quebec) and Nunatsiavut (Northern Labrador)". Inuit Nunangat represents the recognized homeland of Canadian Inuit (Inuit Tapiriit Kanatami n.d.).

7 Institutional awareness and defence of the economic and cultural importance of sealing to Inuit and Indigenous communities as part of the sealing protests of the mid-20th century dates back to at least 1972 in Canada when the Interim Committee on Seals and Sealing acknowledged the dominant NGO messaging being disseminated at that time minimizing the economic importance of sealing for the Canadian economy ignores the fact that "on an individual basis it may represent up to 50% of individual income in a specific geographic area" most especially in the Canadian North and in some rural areas in Atlantic Canada and Quebec (Interim Report to the Minister of Environment from the Committee on Seals and Sealing 1972, 4).

8 The document says that "Jacques Cartier found Labrador Indians taking seals in the Strait of Belle Isle in 1534. Europeans in Newfoundland probably began sealing from shore soon after the discovery of the island and this practice continues to the

present day"; the First Nations peoples of Labrador are the Innu. A large part of Labrador is also the homeland of Inuit.

9   According to the historical work on the seal fishery done by the Department of Fisheries and Oceans Canada in 1979, "[a]fter Newfoundland became a province of Canada in 1949, the Canadian seal hunt became more widely based. Companies were established in Nova Scotia ... hence some of the large vessels which currently take part [but since discontinued] take part in the hunt sail from Nova Scotian ports. However, more of Canada's sealers, past and present, on big ships and small, come from the rugged northeast coast of Newfoundland".

10 2009 is the same year that the European Union extended its ban on seal product imports from Canada to a complete ban on all seal products for commercial sale in the Common Market.

11 Efforts to make the commercial side of sealing more ecologically sustainable have been ongoing for over a century. As far back as 1895, the Dominion of Newfoundland (then self-governing and now the Canadian province of Newfoundland and Labrador) enacting its first laws to try and protect the dwindling seal populations (Farquhar 2020, 14). These laws had limited effect as enforcement was extremely challenging at the time due to the large areas requiring monitoring, technological limitations and a large amount of foreign hunting from vessels based in places like Canada (at that time separate from Newfoundland and Labrador) and Norway. Though the seal population did increase during the Second World War because hunting stopped during this time, it began to decrease again when hunting resumed after the war ended (Hawkins and Silver 2017, 115). Since the 1970s, however, with things like technological changes, monitored quotas and licences, the Northwest Atlantic harp seal population has increased six times its size. As of 2017, "DFO estimates the current Northwest Atlantic harp seal population to be about 7.4 million animals, – six times larger than in the 1970s – and considers the population to be abundant and healthy" (Lafrance 2017).

12 Around the time of the anti-sealing movement, Canada's international maritime boundaries – territorial seas and exclusive economic zones – were changing and this would affect the extent to which Canada would be able to exert control over access to and the protection of the Northwest Atlantic harp seal population. For example, as of "January 1, 1977, Canada proclaimed a 200-mile exclusive fishing zone", and this zone developed into the exclusive economic zone under the Third United Nations Convention on the Law of the Seas (Dale and Mills 1979, 41).

13 There is an Inuit Exception to the European seal product ban, but it limits Inuit imports and does little to help address the overarching stigma impacting the sealing industry and practices which affect all sealers and commercial business regardless of ethnicity.

14 Pockets of discontent against sealing practices from an environmental conservation angle started in the late 1940s and 1950s, but the international awareness of daily sealing practices and issues emerged in earnest following the distribution of a 1964 documentary film about sealing that claimed to show a seal being skinned alive and portrayed the event as though this was the standard practice for killing seals while hunting (CBC Radio 1965; Îles de la Madeleine 2021). The seal skinning, however, was later revealed to be a paid-for stunt by the film crew outside of the sealing season despite being promoted as real activities occurring on the ice during hunt (Burke 2021b). By the time of the revelation, however, public opinion in Europe had already soured against the idea of seal hunting. Animal welfare organizations like the Royal Society for the Prevention of Cruelty to Animals, the Humane Society Canada and IFAW were early leaders in the call for changes to the seal hunt, with Brian Davies, founder of IFAW, being one of the loudest voices, starting with his book *Savage Luxury: The Slaughter of the Baby Seals* (Davies 1970).

15 Like IFAW, PETA also has a long history of concerns about the cruelty of seal hunting and a well-established practice of framing its role against sealing using "a villain-hero-victim narrative that thousands of seals were immorally 'slaughtered' every year. They portrayed seal pups as victims, Atlantic sealers as villains, and [animal rights] groups and those who support their cause as heroes" (Farquhar 2020, 13). However, as public awareness of Indigenous peoples and legal rights, and the legacy of colonialism, has grown in North America and Western Europe and is putting pressure on some environmental and animal rights organizations to blur their concept of cruelty to accommodate hunting provided that the person who kills the seal is Indigenous. PETA now claims to support Indigenous seal hunting, but it displays inconsistencies in its Indigenous sealing support. For example, in an official statement rebutting what PETA views as the failure by others to acknowledge its support for Inuit subsistence hunting, but the organization's headline simultaneously referred to Indigenous hunting as the "Indigenous Seal Slaughter" (PETA n.d.). The use of the word "slaughter" undercuts PETA's display of Indigenous support by continuing to tie the act of sealing with imagery of destruction that the organization has long propagated. According to the Merriam-Webster dictionary, synonyms for slaughter are: (1) as a noun – bloodbath, butchery, carnage, death, holocaust, and massacre; and (2) as a verb – butcher, massacre, and mow (down).

16 The 2020 European Commission report on the trade in seal products, within the EU Finland, for example, has concerns with the current EU regulations noting that it "has gone beyond its intended purpose. The ban has contributed to the present poor state of coastal fishing [in Finland] and significantly downgrading the value of seals as a game species". The report also notes that in Greenland it is believed that the "EU seal regime is having adverse effects on Inuit and other indigenous communities" and in Canada in the Northwest Territories "the direct benefit of the [Inuit/ Indigenous EU ban] exception has been very limited. The attestation costs would be higher than the value of the seal products the system is intended to monitor and certify under the EU Regulation and, therefore, these costs would have to be passed on to the Inuvialuit/Inuit themselves".

17 Paul Watson, founder of Sea Shepherd, started his protests against sealing as a leader within Greenpeace before being expelled for his views and his arguably violence actions in 1977 (Rowsell 1977, 23; Essemlali and Watson 2013; Weyler 2004). Greenpeace's actions and stances against sealing were at their most radical and controversial in 1976–77 while Watson was a member and pushing a strong militant animal rights, no tolerance view against sealing which resulted in his expulsion from Greenpeace as his views were seen to be threatening the organization's reputation and commitment to non-violence protests (Weyler 2004).

18 Narratives are stories and they "are meant to resonate deeply with audiences and help them to make sense of otherwise complex issues" (Farquhar 2020, 14).

19 Another example of a government trying to help improve public understanding about how seals are used is the Government of Newfoundland and Labrador's work disseminating information about efforts to diversify the sealing industry and use of more of the animal beyond the fur, which is a common accusation about the supposed wastefulness of seal hunting (Department of Fisheries and Aquaculture 2012a, 2012b, 2012c in Phelps Bondaroff and Burke 2014).

20 The RSPCA stands for the Royal Society for the Prevention of Cruelty to Animals and the HSC stands for the Humane Society of Canada.

3 Contextualizing the Newfoundland and Labrador Experiences of Anti-Sealing Violence

There are two key things that should be acknowledged to understand the experiences of sealers, their families and communities in Newfoundland and Labrador, and broadly all ethnicities with deeply embedded cultural practices associated with seal hunting in the Canadian Arctic and Northeast (and arguably elsewhere that practice seal hunting like Greenland, Iceland, Finland and Norway), with anti-sealing cultural violence: (1) culture and industry are not interchangeable and (2) subsistence hunting is different from commercial hunting, as previously noted in Chapter 2, though the same individuals may participate in both.[1] Therefore, this chapter explores how culture and industry are intertwined but not interchangeable and the importance of this relationship to understand how sealing is involved in coastal societies in Canada and Newfoundland and Labrador and why this is important historically, culturally and economically. Building on the culture-industry discussion, the chapter elaborates on the complexities of discussing subsistence and commercial seal hunting and experiences with activists given that frequently the same individuals practise both forms of sealing.

Understanding the Nuance of Sealing in Newfoundland and Labrador

In debates about seal hunting, a frequent problem is the generalization – implicitly and explicitly – that an ethnic group's cultural practices of seal hunting[2] and the sealing industry are one and the same. According to Yoshihisa Kashima (2019) "[c]ulture helps human populations adapt to their environments" (Kashima 2019, 151), and as such, culture and market economic practices are not necessarily interchangeable. For hundreds, and in some cases thousands, of years sealing was practised by Indigenous hunters and later early European settlers and their non-Indigenous and mixed race descendants in the Canadian Arctic and Northeast, such as Nunavut, Northwest Territories, Newfoundland and Labrador (Woods 1986; Burke 2021a) and the Quebec North Shore and Magdalen Islands (Fisheries and Oceans Canada 1979; Fisheries and Oceans Canada 2011; Interim Report to the Minister of Environment from the Committee on Seals and Sealing 1972, 4).

DOI: 10.4324/9781003356158-4

It was not until the mid to late 1700s that commercial sealing started (Government of Newfoundland and Labrador n.d.); centuries after Newfoundland and Labrador was first visited by Europeans in 1497 who established seasonal settlements and over a century after the first recorded permanent non-Indigenous settlement in what is now Cupids, Newfoundland in 1610 (Newfoundland and Labrador Tourism 2021). Therefore, while the sealing industry evolved from the environmental adaptation of non-Indigenous and Indigenous peoples to the natural resources available to them, the industry did not supersede the cultures from which it draws its origins and many of its participants.

For starters, it is from the subsistence hunting practices that various approaches to commercial hunting evolved. If we take a strict interpretation of subsistence in Canada for example, personal use licence holders can harvest up to six seals (Fisheries and Oceans Canada 2016; Fisheries and Oceans Canada 1996).[3] Often with subsistence hunting, for example, hunters only have so much personal need for seal pelts/furs. As a result, subsistence hunters may look for opportunities to sell excess seal furs for income to offset the costs associated with hunting, such as fuel for their small boat (if they hunt from boat), insurance and equipment (e.g. safety equipment and bullets) (Burke 2021b, c).

In contrast, commercial sealing was historically a large-scale affair. There could be dozens of vessels (historically known in Newfoundland and Labrador as the sealing fleet) from Newfoundland and Labrador, and elsewhere, harvesting thousands of seals each with the exact number harvested varying yearly and at times having totals for the whole hunting season nearing a million seals (e.g. Murphy 1916). Today commercial sealing is drastically different. Hunters operate from small vessels (longliners), in contrast to the large schooners and steamships of the past, and they catch a few thousand seals each in a season, with the overall haul of seals for the season across the industry depending on factors such as the size of the seal herd, government set quotas, market demand and ice conditions.[4]

For example, Fisheries and Oceans Canada (2011) reported that the number of seal pelts (mainly harp seals) landed in Canada for commercial purposes is in steady decline with approximately 67000 pelts harvested in 2010, for example. The 2010 quota reflects a steep decline in harvests since the mid-2000s: 2004 (362000 pelts); 2005 (316000); 2006 (348000); 2007 (224000); 2008 (215000); 2009 (91000); and 2010 (67000) (Fisheries and Oceans Canada 2011).[5] However, organizations against seal hunting like The Humane Society of the United States (2022) provide potentially misleading claims on their website that "[i]n recent years, hundreds of thousands of seals have been killed annually in the [Canadian] commercial seal hunt. More than one million seals have been slaughtered in the past five years alone". While it has proven difficult to confirm the Humane Society's claims due to the open-endedness of numbers like "hundreds of thousands" and the lack of current seal harvest numbers since 2010 from Fisheries and Oceans Canada, the trends from 2004 to 2010 marked an exponential decline in seals killed annually in Canada (Fisheries and Oceans Canada 2011). Furthermore, another indication of the decline in seals killed in Canada is that there has been a freeze on the issuing of new commercial seal hunting licences (Fisheries and Oceans Canada 2016).

Lastly, IFAW claims on its website that it, in conjunction with European politicians, has been able to bring about a 90 percent decrease in the number of sealers (IFAW n.d.). The IFAW claims that both the 21st-century trend in Canada of decreasing seals killed annually and the lack of new licences to permit commercial seal harvesting suggest that either the veracity of the Humane Society's claims requires re-evaluation on the part of the organization or the IFAW needs to re-consider how it came up with its 90 percent claim to represent the number of sealers is has removed from the industry.

Additionally, at the same time as the number of seals being killed annually has decreased, according to Fisheries and Oceans Canada's numbers, the seals in the Northwest Atlantic herd have expanded to be "six times larger than in the 1970s" (Lafrance 2017). It is common for many of the same individuals who are subsistence hunters to participate in commercial sealing due to access to sealing opportunities, the required skillsets to practise sealing correctly and legally, and the fact that commercial sealing is part of the seasonal fishing economic structure of many fishing communities in the Canadian Northeast.

The reality is, however, that many non-Indigenous sealers have both commercial and personal use licences. This means that while they may hunt commercially as part of their employment as a fisher, they also hunt for personal consumption. In reality sealers – commercial and subsistence/personal use – do not adhere to the persistent stereotype that they only take the fur of the animal and leave the rest of it on the ice. This is an antiquated idea based on historical commercial sealing practices in the 1800s and early-mid 1900s due to the limited export market for seal meat and the inability to effectively and safely store large quantities of raw meat offshore while hunting (Phelps Bondaroff and Burke 2014). Commercial sealing is very different in the 21st century. While sealers still collect the commercially viable parts of the animal to sell, mainly the fur for international markets, technological changes in vessel refrigeration and the move toward small vessels and market diversification enable fishers/sealers to keep other parts such as meat, like the flippers which are a delicacy in Newfoundland and Labrador and the whole carcass to make items like stew meat and sausages, for personal consumption or local sale.[6] Other parts of the animal for export, such as seal penis which is a common export to Asian markets for use in traditional medicine, are becoming more common as market opportunities for seal products expand beyond the historical European markets (e.g. CBC News 2009; also see Phelps Bondaroff and Burke 2014).

When the anti-sealing movement started in the mid-20th century, little effort was made to distinguish between sealing/fishing cultures and their personal use/subsistence practices and the sealing industry as a whole, nor how the two broad forms of seal hunting are historically and culturally intertwined. Activists from organizations like the IFAW and Greenpeace rose to international prominence in the 1970s–1980s by focusing on the idea that sealing is morally wrong, inherently questioning the moral legitimacy of sealing practices and cultures (Patey 1990; Phelps Bondaroff and Burke 2014). Efforts to distinguish between commercial and subsistence sealing were limited which compounded the negative experiences of local peoples and cultures that were harmed in the process of the protests (Kerr 2014; Patey 1990; Phelps Bondaroff and Burke 2014).

Greenpeace Canada, however, has notably softened some of its stance on sealing, acknowledging its role in some of the issues that it, and allies at the time, caused. In 2014 Greenpeace Canada made a public apology to Inuit, Indigenous and coastal peoples stating that:

> Like the corporations we campaign against, we too must be open to change. Open to examining ourselves, our history, and the impact our campaigns have had, and to constantly reassessing ourselves – not just by apologizing, but by humbly making amends and changing the way we work. And we have a responsibility – not just as an organization that once campaigned against the commercial hunt, but also as conscious, socially responsible human beings – to right wrongs, to actively stop the spread of misinformation, and to decolonize our thinking, our language and our approach.
>
> (Kerr 2014)

Greenpeace also acknowledges that its conduct, and that of the anti-sealing movement, muddled messaging about commercial sealing versus subsistence hunting, the latter of which they initially supported, and are again expressing some degree of acceptance for. The result of the anti-sealing campaigning, as Greenpeace Canada now recognizes, is irreparable damage to the peoples and cultures connected to sealing practices (Kerr 2014).[7]

Jessica Wilson, a Greenpeace member who worked for Greenpeace Canada as part its cooperation with the Nunavut Inuit community Kanngiqtugaapik/Clyde River in the mid-2010s and its appeal against seismic testing for non-renewable resources near the community, acknowledges that for many peoples in the Canadian North Greenpeace's anti-sealing campaign has come to define it in the region (also see Burke 2021d).

> The image for it for many people up North is that it is kind of all Greenpeace. The leadership at the time had quite a diversion of opinion on the seal campaign. Once they had gone up to the north and met with some Inuit and started to understand impacts of their campaign Bob Hunter and Paul Watson started to have a difference of opinion over this

that led, in a lot of ways, to the creation of Sea Shepherd. Paul Watson left the organization. Bob Hunter wanted to go, what he called "deep green"; less about animal rights and more about the notion of true ecology, which involves humans. It was one of the founders, Bob Hunter I think, said, "Ecology, look it up! You're in it!"

(Interview with Jessica Wilson of
Greenpeace Canada 2018)

The organization's limited effort to date to acknowledge the extent of its role in the anti-sealing protests and the colonial approach of activists toward Inuit, Indigenous and coastal peoples will take a long time and care for it to navigate successfully (Kerr 2014; also see Burke 2020). Greenpeace Canada is presently trying to express regret for past actions and attitudes expressed during its time in the anti-sealing movement in Canada in the 1970s and 1980s, but also wants to maintain the organization's stance against commercial sealing (Burgwald 2016). The organization also has an unclear position on the extent of its contrition toward non-Indigenous cultures harmed by anti-sealing protestors, like the people of Newfoundland and Labrador whom the organization intentionally targeted during its anti-sealing campaigning (Burke 2022b; 2021c; also see CBC The Broadcast with Jane Adey 2021).[8]

However, other organizations, like IFAW and Sea Shepherd, still view sealing as immoral and illegitimate and argue strongly against seal hunting. IFAW, for example, strives for an end to all commercial sealing (IFAW 2020) and has worked with EU members of parliament to oppose seal hunting on ethical grounds (IFAW n.d.). IFAW boasts on its website that it has reduced the number of sealers in Canada by 90 percent as a result of its work to get import bans imposed in Europe (IFAW n.d.).

IFAW's current stance against all commercial sealing is not new. The organization was also founded in 1969 by Brian Davies with the explicit purpose to fight commercial sealing along the Northeast Coast of Canada and the organization is very proud of its anti-sealing history (IFAW 2019). As part of its work against sealing, for example, IFAW ran a major information campaign in Europe and the United States by hiring the same public relations firm as Coca-Cola in 1974 (McKibbon 2000). It took actions such as media stunts and news stories, public film screenings selectively portraying the seal hunt, protests, pamphlet mailing and protest mail-in letters to local and European Economic Community (EEC) politicians calling for a ban on sealing (Woods 1986).

In the end, European politicians implemented its first seal product ban on whitecoat harp seal pelts in 1983 (European Commission 2019a). Later the European market ban expanded into an outright ban on all seal product imports imposed by the EEC successor, the European Union (EU), in 2009. The EU ban, however, has a limited exception for Indigenous/Inuit subsistence-hunted seal products (European Commission 2019b). In response to IFAW's continued anti-sealing campaigning and its influence in motivating the EU to ban commercial seal product imports, then Inuit Tapiriit Kanatami president Mary Simon, now Governor General of Canada, stated in 2010: "No objective and fair minded person can conclude that seals are under genuine conservation threat or that Inuit hunting activities are less humane than those practiced by hunting communities all over the world, including hunters in Europe" (Phillips 2010).

In the case of Newfoundland and Labrador, it is both the front line of anti-sealing activism and home to the sealers and communities there were most famously targeted in an asymmetrical power struggle over the world's conceptualization of sealing as a practice and as the basis of an industry (Patey 1990). Local sealers, communities and supporters were forced to try and defend themselves against what is now a well-established stigma that portrays them as indiscriminate killers and slaughters (e.g. Sea Shepherd 2021). James Winter has been working on elevating the voices of sealers since 1977 when he was an embedded CBC journalist with sealers on the ice in 1977 and 1978 doing participant observation of the hunt for the broadcaster. In his experience Winter observed activists and their national and international media and donor supporters conduct "vicious propaganda campaigns attacking basically defenceless rural people" (Interview with James Winter 2021 - see Burke 2022a).

When Newfoundland and Labrador sealers tried to defend themselves, anti-sealing advocates provoked responses so they could point to sealers and portray them as the violent, uneducated and uncivilized actors (Patey 1990). For example, Paul Watson in 1977 (then of Greenpeace) came to rural Newfoundland and proceeded to reportedly threaten to beat sealers with their own clubs and threw seal pelts and equipment into water (e.g. Nagtzaam et al. 2019; also see Patey 1990 for more on the local experience with protesters like Paul Watson and Brian Davies in Newfoundland). Winter recalls that when he transitioned from working as a journalist covering the anti-sealing protests to becoming what he describes as a human rights campaigner on behalf of the traditional cultural and economic rights of sealers, their families and communities in the Canadian Northeast and Arctic, few in the media or European or American political class were interested in hearing about the cultural violence that rural working-class sealers were experiencing. Winter also expressed that in his experience:

> What I witnessed made me think seriously about what was happening. Mercenary ego driven corporations creating a fallacy that enjoyed the support of careless, if not deliberately misleading, journalism sold to a worldwide urban audience…We had no money and no organization, and no interest in our story from the media.
>
> (Interview with James Winter 2021 - see Burke 2022a)

More recently, Newfoundland documentary filmmaker Anne Troake was targeted by anti-sealing activists and experienced death threats, stalking, harassment and property damage for making the film *My Ancestors Were Rogues and Murderers* in 2005. In an interview I conducted with Troake (Burke 2023) she recalls that after the release of her documentary film:

> I received phone calls in the middle of the night issuing death threats and in one case a man called repeatedly and just growled. One night a car pulled up in front of my home and someone threw a brick through my window.

Furthermore Troake recounted that

> [m]embers of the Sea Shepherd Society in particular, wrote some hateful *ad hominem* responses in internet chat spaces [about Troake and her documentary]. This was still in the early days of social media, and doxing [publishing personal information about people with malicious intent] had not emerged as the commonplace phenomenon it is today. Paul Watson called me "inbred", said that Newfoundlanders debased Canada when we joined the country and compared sealers to the soldiers of the Third Reich. I am also aware that Newfoundland sealers have been described by another leading activist as malignantly inbred, sadistic, cowardly wastes of human skin, and my film as pure fantasy.
> (Interview with Anne Troake 2022 - see Burke 2023)

Notably Sea Shepherd, the organization that Troake spoke about, states that it is a practitioner of non-violence (Sea Shepherd n.d.). However, Troake's experience with Sea Shepherd activists raises a serious point about how organizations and their members and supporters interpret non-violence and what their boundaries are for acceptable actions, attitudes and behaviours in pursuit of their causes.

The navigation in activism and the concept of peaceful protests, which Greenpeace for example also argues is core to its practices, philosophy and identity (Greenpeace International 2018, 3–4; Greenpeace International 2020), is blurry when reflecting on the activism of its anti-sealing legacy. It harkens back to Johan Galtung's (1990) point on experiences of cultural violence and the use of siege and sanctions tactics to try and force an outcome under the guise of non-violence: "To some, this is 'non-violence', since direct and immediate killing is avoided. To the victims ... the actor avoids having to face the violence directly ... meaning the loss of freedom and identity instead of loss of life and limbs" for those targeted (1990, 293).

According to Patrick Moore, former president of Greenpeace and an active anti-sealing protester for the organization in the 1970s–1980s before his controversial expulsion from the organization in 1986:

> peacefulness, passivism is non-violence, but it doesn't include inciting other people to violence against you. That is not passivism. In other

words, by you making the first blow, or you chaining yourself to some-
one's tractor who is trying to make a living with it, that is not peaceful
… it is not peaceful to interfere with other peoples' livelihoods in a way
that threatens their livelihoods. That's not peaceful.

(Moore 2021).

While Moore's comment was not made in the context of the sealing protests,
his reflection on non-violence more broadly is interesting because "[o]ne way
cultural violence works is by changing the moral color of an act from red/
wrong to green/right or at least to yellow/acceptable" (Galtung 1990, 292).
The creative use of activist framing such as describing their work as based in
non-violence/nonviolence strategies and tactics, for example, while simultaneously using ethnics and cultural slurs to stigmatized and devalue traditional
groups and practices plays into the redefining of moral boundaries and nor-
malizing processes and outcomes that would otherwise be seen as questionable, if not downright problematic.

Presently, the dominant public national and international narratives about
sealing are largely one-sided against sealers. As a result, the violence experienced by sealers and their families in places like Newfoundland and Labrador
has become concealed "by making reality opaque so that we do not see the
violent act or fact, or at least not as violent" (Galtung 1990, 292). This con-
cealment limits dissenting voices from being taken seriously by media and
decision-makers by eliminating nuance about a subject, in this case sealing as
the Western moral colouring of what is acceptable to say, do and support with
regard to sealing has largely been set by activist opinions and recollections of
past and current events.

Despite more recent allowances to acknowledge Inuit traditional sealing
rights (e.g. Kerr 2014; PETA n.d.), the moral colouring of violence against
sealers undermines Inuit/Indigenous peoples by pigeon-holing good versus
bad hunting to limit Inuit to a strict interpretation of subsistence-level hunting, and erasing non-Indigenous traditional practices and cultures at the same
time. As Troake pointedly observed about the problematic framing of morally
acceptable versus unacceptable sealers and sealing practices:

[t]he implication of an action being morally acceptable for one racial
or ethnic group and not for another is both troubling and, in this case,
ironic. This sort of arbitrary moral division is reminiscent of the original
rationale for colonizing what is now known as the Americas.

(Interview with Anne Troake 2022 - see Burke 2023)

Overall, moralizing on acceptable hunting through stigmatizing alterna-
tives beyond traditional Indigenous subsistence hunting exerts control over
Indigenous self-determination by affecting the ability of Indigenous nations to
expand their economic opportunities using the natural resources available in

their homelands. It also puts a choke-hold on non-Indigenous sealing cultural practices by erasing their existence and significance with the aim of gradually suffocating them into endangered status, if not outright extinction.

Notes

1 Please note that this author fully acknowledges the impact of the anti-sealing movement on Indigenous peoples in Canada with peoples such as Canadian Inuit in the Northwest Territories and Nunavut, which was disproportionately worse economically compared to coastal peoples in the Canadian Northeast as a result of the substantial market impact of sanctions and the stigmatization of seal products in the 1970s–1980s, the large percentage of the economy that sealing played in many Inuit communities in the Canadian Arctic and more limited opportunities for economic diversification for Inuit communities when the impact of the protests and sanctions came into effect (Woods 1986; Phelps Bondaroff and Burke 2014). Indigenous experiences in Canada are also compounded by more extreme experiences with colonialism which has a complex influence and impact on Canadian society and attitudes, and which are acknowledged by Greenpeace Canada, for example, for playing a significant role on the attitudes, actions and behaviours of the anti-sealing campaigners on and toward their level of consideration about the repercussions of their activities on Canadian Inuit, Indigenous peoples and coastal peoples (Kerr 2014). Overarching, however, this book argues that there are elements of a broadly shared experiences of having faced cultural violence between Indigenous and non-Indigenous sealers and their families in Newfoundland and Labrador and the Canadian Inuit, for example, due to wider societal ignorance about their cultures, economies and histories as they relate to sealing; deliberate mis- and under-representations of their viewpoints on sealing and the impact of the protests, stigmatization and sanctions by media and protesters; and a complex history of identity inclusion and tolerance within Canadian society as a result of being distinct nations within the Canadian Confederation.

2 It is vital to note that there are different cultures in Canada to which the issue of sealing cultural practices/heritage is part of what makes the groups distinct. Arguably the easiest ethnic groups to associate with sealing cultural practices are also racially (and visibly) distinct from majority populations such as Inuit and some First Nations such as Innu and Mi'kmaq. However, other broader ethnic groups exist too such as Newfoundlanders (the concept of Newfoundlanders as an ethnic group is explained further in Chapter 4; also see Smith 2017; Baker 2014; Clarke 2012) that have a strong cultural, economic and historical connection to sealing. It is also important to acknowledge that many individuals have mixed ancestry and may identify as members of more than one ethnic group, such as seeing oneself as Mi'kmaw and as a Newfoundlander, for example. The group to which an individual identifies with most strongly may also be context dependent. On the topic of the harm caused to Newfoundland and Labrador by anti-sealing activists, for example, an individual may identify more strongly with their cultural connection and collective experience as a Newfoundlander since they were intentionally targeted by protesters on the basis of this identity, but on a different subject such as contemporary economic development proposals in the province (e.g. wind energy), they may identify more strongly with their Mi'kmaw ethnicity as it pertains to issues such as economic benefits sharing and the duty to consult local peoples in their particular part of the province. As James Baker (2014) acknowledges in his work on Newfoundland ethnicity, the concept of ethnicity is complex, complicated and contested. It is this author's point, therefore, to highlight the nuances of a subject

like cultural violence and anti-sealing protests in a place like Newfoundland and Labrador which are difficult to fully condense because many people with deep cultural and ethnic roots in the province hold different identities simultaneously that may be affected in different ways as a result of the conduct of anti-sealing protesters and the outcomes they precipitated. For example, an individual and their family may have experienced the direct and indirect repercussions of anti-sealing violence as targets for stigmatization, devaluation and attack because they were identifiable as Newfoundlanders or Labradorians who participated in and/or supported the seal hunt and sealing practices, but their individual experiences of cultural violence at the hands of protesters and their supporters may be compounded by the fact that they are also Indigenous (e.g. Mi'kmaw), and their Indigenous heritage and how it informs their sealing cultural practices and traditions have been largely ignored for much of the decades-long sealing debate.

3 To obtain a personal use licence, hunters must undergo training provided by Fisheries and Oceans Canada. Furthermore, "[n]o person shall fish (hunt) for pups" and must be over 18 years old. There is also a freeze (as of 2016) on the issuing of new harp seal licences (Fisheries and Oceans Canada 2016).

4 This broad information about the change in how sealing is conducted at the industry level was obtained from a conversation with a former Fisheries and Oceans Canada fisheries officer who once monitored the seal hunt in the 1970s and worked on fisheries issues in rural and coastal Newfoundland and Labrador for over 30 years. This conversation is not for direct quotation or attribution, but to give an overview of how things changed from the historical image of what the seal hunt was at the turn of the 20th century to what it has become by the dawn of the 21st century.

5 The numbers for 2008–2010 years are based on preliminary data.

6 For example, local independent butchers and fish trucks in Newfoundland and Labrador often sell seal products such as the flippers and carcass as this author can attest. As a Newfoundlander, I can and have gone to a local butcher in my part of the province and purchased fresh seal meat and products which are available seasonally.

7 Greenpeace Nordic has also worked to build bridges with Greenlandic Inuit since the 2010s as part of the organization's regional efforts to reconcile their relationships with Arctic Indigenous peoples as a result of Greenpeace's leading role in the anti-sealing movement and its very negative effects on Inuit rights and economies (Burke 2020). For example, according to Faiza Outahsen of Greenpeace based in the Netherlands, who has worked extensively for the organization on its Arctic strategizing and campaigning: "I do know that when we started to develop the campaign on the Arctic, we defined particular strands of strategy. We also looked back at what was the campaigning we did in the past relating to [the] Arctic. The seal campaign was obviously a big [one], and so was the whaling campaign … we did play a role in creating this image which impacted these communities and I would say there is no doubt about it. It is also very right that Greenpeace apology for that several times. And you definitely see a lot of anger about that in Canadian communities, some Canadian communities. Greenland [too, there's] no doubt about it" (Interview with Faiza Outahsen of Greenpeace Netherlands, 2018).

8 Greenpeace was instrumental in setting the trend of celebrity endorsements of the anti-sealing cause, starting with French actress Brigitte Bardot in 1977 (Greenpeace 1977; also see Patey 1990).

4 The Newfoundland and Labrador Anti-Sealing Movement Experience

This chapter explores how activism against seal hunting devolved into cultural violence against sealers, their families and communities in Newfoundland and Labrador. Drawing on archival research from the Centre for Newfoundland Studies, Memorial University of Newfoundland and Labrador, in addition to supplementary interviews, this chapter illustrates how the Newfoundland and Labrador experiences with anti-sealing protesters escalated to the normalization of cultural violence in the 1970s–1980s as a means to destabilize the sealing industry and groups associated with it.

The chapter argues that the rural and coastal Newfoundland and Labrador experience with anti-sealing protesters amounts to cultural violence as the techniques used by activists over decades based on five dimensions of cultural violence distilled from the literature: (1) inflictors of violence believe they are operating from a place of moral authority; (2) the attackers are identifiably distinct from the group(s) they are targeting; (3) the instances of violence are unidirectional; (4) the targets of violence are immobile; and (5) the actions and attitudes are pushing people into forced assimilation (e.g. Belsky and Klagsbrun 2018; Campbell 2009; Kingston 2015; also see Burke 2021b, c). Much of the focus is on the height of the anti-sealing protests in the 1970s and 1980s which has had long-term effects on framing global perceptions about sealing and sealers. The following sections address the above five characteristics with some of these characteristics being addressed together – the attackers are identifiably distinct from the group(s) targeted with forced assimilation and unidirectional violence with immobility of targets. These dimensions are explored together because they are closely tied when discussing the experiences of cultural violence in Newfoundland and Labrador. This chapter argues that over the years anti-sealing activists and their supporters have created and encouraged an implicitly pursued and fostered overarching campaign of cultural violence against Newfoundland and Labrador sealers through attitudes, actions and behaviours that have blurred the lines of morality and acceptable conduct toward disproportionately weaker rural and coastal sealers, their families and communities. Reported experiences in rural and coastal Newfoundland and Labrador that have arguably contributed to the outcome of cultural violence, and which are explored in more detail in this chapter, include: anonymous threats to kidnap and skin local children of

DOI: 10.4324/9781003356158-5

sealers to pressure parents to abandon their cultural and economic practices; swarming of rural coastal communities by protester and media; in at least one documented instance, protesters reportedly holding a sealer hostage on a floating ice pan while verbally and psychologically abusing him; deliberately equating Newfoundland and Labrador's centuries-old sealing culture and economic practices to misrepresent the role of sealing and the sealing industry in the Canadian economy; and pushing for the assimilation of Newfoundlanders and Labradorians into becoming "Canadian".

Inflictors of Violence and Self-Appointed Moral Authorities

For non-state actors to effectively do their work they "must encourage outsiders of the legitimacy of their cause(s), often without the benefit of nationalism or other existing cultural or moral resources" (Lowe 2008, 71). Organizations like IFAW, PETA and Greenpeace sought to legitimatize their work against sealing by taking the moral position that hunting is wrong (Randhawa 2017) and set about crafting narratives to support this position. The narratives were crafted and communicated in many ways including through media coverage, films/documentaries, newsletters and petitions (Patey 1990), but the environmental organizations rarely distributed images that portrayed the negative impacts they were having on local peoples. Rather their "[s]kilful manipulation of the mass media engender[ed] enormous sympathy for their cause" (Kalland 2009, 82).

Greenpeace stands out in this discussion because when it originally protested against what it argued was the unsustainability of the sealing industry starting in 1976, it initially recognized the cultural importance of sealing for Inuit and Newfoundland and Labrador (Burke 2021c).

> The fact is that the commercial fleets owned by Norwegian companies are wiping out the seal herds. The fact is the Norwegians destroyed three great herds of seals prior to starting on the Labrador herds in 1947. The fact is that the commercial fleets take only the pelts, leaving the meat on the ice, while the fishermen and [Inuit] of Newfoundland and Labrador do eat the meat. With a conservation stand the seals could have a chance.
> (Greenpeace Chronicles 1976, 6 as quoted in Harter 2004, 96)

Quickly, however, Greenpeace abandoned its nuanced approach and focused on pushing for an end to all sealing, or what they considered to be "the savage, uncontrolled slaughter of helpless baby seals for their white pelts" (Woods 1986, 2). The organization deliberately tied the sealing debate to questions about the value of the sealing industry to the Canadian economy because the average sealers earned returns of around 100–200 CAD (in 1970s–early

1980s) off pelts from animals killed for family/personal use (Greenpeace Foundation 1977).

Paul Watson was instrumental in Greenpeace's rapid move away from nuance on the sealing issue. Watson promoted extreme action against sealers and sealing communities leading to "increased publicity and, subsequently, more donations for Greenpeace" (Nagtzaam et al. 2019). However, Rex Weyler, a former leader in Greenpeace, noted that "Watson tended to push the end of non-violence" which put Greenpeace into a difficult position as Watson's stances and actions undermined Greenpeace position that it was a non-violent organization. As a result the "Greenpeace Foundation board censured and removed Watson by a vote of 11-1, his being the dissenting vote" (Weyler 2004, 457), though Watson contends that his work was non-violent and justified (Essemlali and Watson 2013).

Greenpeace, however, has not offered an explicit and public apology to Newfoundland and Labrador sealers, their families and communities for the violence they experienced while targeted by their organization and its supporters (Burke 2021c). Rather there is a subtle, implicit and somewhat vague possible inclusion of Newfoundlanders and Labradorians under the broad category of coastal peoples in Greenpeace's 2014 apology. However, the 2014 apology lacks specifics about different coastal peoples in Canada and only highlights Inuit in Canada for any detailed reference in the apology (Kerr 2014).

Anti-sealing protesters also downplayed and largely ignored that "the seal hunt is an integral part of the seasonal fishing cycle for most of the longliner operations in northern Newfoundland and is absolutely essential to the economic viability of many vessels in the fleet" (Sinclair et al. 1989, 35) and that "in a rural economy with so few opportunities to earn cash, even these small amounts may take on a social significance far greater than for most urban dwellers" (Sinclair et al. 1989, 29). As Wright (1981, p. 62) notes, protesters preferred to focus on their interpretation of the "material viability of the hunt" in order "to argue that since the seal hunt adds only about $5 500 000 ... to the total economy of the province, it cannot have a claim as an important or vital part of the economy" while underplaying the "culturally meaningful aspect of sealing".

The income from the commercial sealing in some coastal fishing communities, for example, accounted for 30–50 per cent of the income for those that operated the longliners in the 1970s and early 1980s (Royal Commission on Seals and the Sealing Industry in Canada, Volume 1, Economic Options, Prospects and Issues 1986, 4), and still does for some fishers (Troake 2005). There are also knock-on effects of removing 30–50 per cent of a person's income, for individuals, their families and communities which can have major societal and cultural implications which have been largely unacknowledged in the whole sealing debate.

The negative economic impacts of undermining inshore sealing necessitates greater dependence on summer tourism, which, on the surface might appear relatively benign, but it forces our communities into a dependence on global mobility and its entwinement with fossil fuel use as well as casting us and our towns in a performative role wherein we must also depend on fulfilling the curiosity and comfort requirements of vacationers. So on one hand, the loss of sealing serves up more desperate workers to Big Industry and on the other, it casts rural Newfoundlanders and Labradorians as the Piper in the old adage: He who pays the piper calls the tune. We lose members of our communities to migrant work and we are dependent on the interest of tourists in consuming a commoditized version of our culture.

(Interview with Anne Troake 2022 - see Burke 2023)

In contemporary times,

[t]he average harvester earns only 20-35% of his yearly income – a meager $5,000 to 8,000 – from sealing, and relies on other work to survive. A vast majority of sealers come from Canada's poorest, most isolated regions and have few alternatives for work (Crockett 2015).

A key part of the approach of many frontline anti-sealing actors, like Greenpeace, was to stage direct action opportunities and image events for maximum media and promotional material coverage and impact directly against hunting by targeting sealers on the ice or in their isolated and rural communities. According to Link and Phelan (2001, 375) "[s]tigma is entirely dependent on social, economic, and political power – it takes power to stigmatize". Greenpeace, for example, knew that many of the people participating in the seal fishery had an average "3.5 dependents, [and] an average education of grade 9, living in isolated communities with limited occupational mobility" according to a Greenpeace report from 1977 (Greenpeace Foundation 1977, 2), so it is reasonable to argue that they knew that the likelihood of the individuals they were targeting would be able to mount an effective defence of their culture and practices against what the activist organizations were doing at a global scale was very low on the basis of resources, skills and access to opportunities.

Instead, sealers and their communities were inundated with protesters and media who attacked them in their homes and while they were out hunting; there was no escape for them and their families.

The legacy of the anti-sealing activists is that emotional propaganda defeats facts, that ignorance trumps knowledge, and that media can be manipulated to become your PR arm. For sealers and their families the victimization exists every day. We are unlikely to see any change in this attitude while governments, institutions, individuals, and media accept fiction over fact.

(Interview with James Winter 2021 - see Burke 2022a)

Activists pushed narratives of brave protesters against savage peasants. Anne Troake recalls in her documentary on her family's experience with the protesters and their view of Newfoundlanders and Labradorians: "Some say we are lazy. Others say we are savages" (Troake 2005). Leaders in the protests such as Brian Davies of IFAW and Paul Watson of Sea Shepherd (formerly of Greenpeace) wrote passionately about their work against sealing, for example (e.g. Davis 1970; Essemlali and Watson 2013; also see Weyler 2004).

Regardless of the longevity and importance of sealing in Newfoundland and Labrador, and in many coastal areas of the Canadian Arctic and Northeast, protesters and their supporters levelled repeated personal attacks, bigotry, xenophobia and threats of physical harm against sealers for decades (e.g. Patey 1990; Roswell 1977; Felsberg 1985). In some cases, the vitriol and calls for physical violence and the promotion of psychological and cultural violence against sealers continue to be supported by anti-sealing activists (CBC News 2005a, b). Watson, for example, expressed support in 2005 for a Sea Shepherd board member – Jerry Vlasak – who has reportedly "endorsed assassination as a means to save animal life" and has participated in direct action during the Canadian seal hunt (CBC News 2005a, b).

At the height of the anti-sealing movement in the mid-1970s, Newfoundland and Labrador sealers had limited support and recourse when trying to deal with national and international media coverage, letters and telephone calls filled with hatred. Francis Patey of St. Anthony, Newfoundland, was at the heart of the local effort to protect Newfoundland and Labrador during the anti-sealing movement. In his book, *A Battle Lost*, Patey reproduces copies of some of the letters received by local sealers which included things like: "murderers, may you be damned from here to eternity!" (Patey 1990, 62); "You people of Newfoundland are a bunch of murderers ... I guess it's true, Newfoundland IS backward, ignorant and prehistoric" (1990, 56); "If [killing seals] is the only way these men can make a living, I hope they all starve to death. Better still, maybe we could CLUB them to death" (1990, 55);

> You dirty, rotten son-of-a-bitch! If I could get to you, I would beat you senseless; then I would skin your hide. You are a mean bastard and you will pay for your sins. You're lucky I don't go up there now and do it. I hope you die. Don't be surprised if you hear me or see me ... I'd pay anything to have you for five minutes";
>
> (1990, 50)

"You Murdering Bastards" (1990, 53); and "I have heard you are tired of being called murderers, but if the shoe fits, wear it! ... It is unfortunate that the world is populated with money-hungry people like your gang" (1990, 52–3).

Threats designed to dissuade people in Newfoundland and Labrador from practice or supporting their cultural sealing traditions or participating in commercial sealing continue to this day. In one case in the mid-2010s, for example, a Newfoundland woman whose father is a sealer reportedly received "a threat to kidnap and skin her three-year-old child after she posted a photo of them wearing a seal-fur bow tie and hat" in order to simulate how the anti-sealing supporter believes seals are killed (Burke 2021b; also see CBC The Broadcast with Jane Adey 2021). When considering that leading anti-sealing advocates like Watson have expressed support for a member of his organization who is reportedly fine with the idea to assassinate people to protect animals (CBC News 2005a, b), threats to kidnap, torture and kill children to promote the anti-sealing case are taken very seriously and terrify sealers and their families in Newfoundland and Labrador, such as the mother in this example (CBC The Broadcast with Jane Adey 2021).

In the 1970s–1980s, a way of thinking began to emerge within the environmental movement that humans are the environment's problem, which helps to explain why the demonization, abuse and dehumanization of sealers quickly became normalized and still has a strong following to this day. Patrick Moore, the controversial former Greenpeace President reflected that:

> by the time I left [Greenpeace]…the environmental movement had changed … [it turned] to "humans are the enemies of the Earth" "humans are the enemies of nature" as if we're the only bad or evil species on the planet and everything else is either benign or good or whatever you want to say. They're not evil. This is original sin reinvented for environmentalism.
>
> (Moore 2021)[1]

When people operate from a position that their work is essential to eradicate original sin, then any people, actors or cultures that they perceive to be in the way of fulfilling their calling are likely to be viewed as transgressors to be converted or eliminated in some fashion. In the case of the anti-sealing protesters, the discourse around calls to reform the sealing industry very rapidly shifted away from conservation and sustainable use of seals became drowned out as calls for an outright ban of all sealing became to dominate the debate (Phelps Bondaroff and Burke 2014).[2] Anyone or any culture between the followers of the anti-sealing cause and their objectives risk being stigmatized as unworthy and subhuman; a status of being less-than that underpins questionable actions, attitudes and behaviours toward vulnerable peoples and cultures in this case.

Attackers Are Identifiably Distinct From Their Targets and Forced Assimilation

According to Sinclair et al. in a *Report for the Royal Commission on Seals and the Sealing Industry in Canada* (1989):

Sealing takes place in Canada's most marginal or peripheral regions, and the fact that commercial utilization of seal products has declined so dramatically in recent years is a threat to the very existence of some of Canada's most isolated settlements. Consequently, it is important to evaluate sealing not in relation to its contribution to Canadian society as a whole, but with reference to the general resources and economic condition of the regions in which sealing takes place.

(Sinclair et al. 1989, 2)

Anti-sealing advocates, however, have long framed sealing as an antiquated practice in Canadian history (McDermott 1985, 2) in which the Canadian majority are now against (Scheffer 1984, 4).

By blurring the lines between the wider Canadian economy and the importance of sealing to specific cultural and ethnically distinct segments of Canada operating within that economy, activists used "taken-for-granted cultural circumstances" (Link and Phelan 2014, 24). In this case the taken-for-granted circumstance is that the sealers are Canadian. The Canadian framing blocks out any ethnic or cultural nuances that also identify who these sealers and their families are beyond the very broad "Canadian" classification. By eradicating nuance, protesters distort the discussion about the economic benefits of sealing to Canadian society and the cultural importance of sealing traditions and practices to sub-sets of cultural and ethnically distinct peoples who also happen to be Canadian citizens.

The eradication of nuance about the peoples who make up Canada and Canadians is particularly prevalent in the sealing debate and the experiences of Newfoundlanders and Labradorians who have long been stigmatized in Canada as "less-than" while also being culturally, and arguably ethnically, distinct (see Baker 2014 for exploration of Newfoundland [and Labrador] ethnicity).

From the beginning the anti-sealing movement focused on Newfoundland and Labrador … . The anti-sealing corporations fully understood the political and cultural reality in Canada towards Newfoundland and Labrador as the new province versus the established province of Quebec. Also in Canada this was the era of the "Newfie joke" and the establishment of the concept of Newfoundlanders and Labradoreans as being stupid, redneck, and somehow not deserving of being considered as "Canadian". As a tactic it worked for a couple of decades helping the propaganda to influence Canadian, and to a degree international, thought.

(Interview with James Winter 2021 - see Burke 2022a)

However, sealing means more for rural and coastal Newfoundland and Labrador culture and society than its role as an economic enterprise.[3] Sealing created a culture and a working-class solidarity among the sealing communities with "[t]he class formation of sealers…[differing] from the more typical development of waged workers in Canada" (Harter 2004, 94).

In the case of Newfoundland and Labrador, the location from which the majority of sealing in Canada takes place, the peoples of the province were essentially Canadian immigrants when the protests against them began, having only joining Canada in 1949 (Cochrane and Parsons 1949).[4] Anti-sealing activists in the late 1960s–1980s came from outside of the province and attacked the traditional ways of life and economic practices of rural and coastal peoples of Newfoundland and Labrador who are ethnically and culturally distinct from the people who they attacked (e.g. Burke 2021c; Baker 2014; Harter 2004).[5]

While it is easy to comprehend the cultural, ethnic and racial differences between the largely non-Indigenous protesters and Inuit peoples, for example, Newfoundland and Labrador was a separate country that joined Canada, and the Newfoundlanders and Labradorians (and their descendants) at the time of Confederation in 1949 are also culturally and ethnically distinct people. According to James Baker and his work on Newfoundland ethnicity, ethnicity

> is very much at the core of the individual; in fact, ethnic identity can influence how we perceive both ourselves and others … . Loosely speaking, an ethnic group is defined as a group of people whose members identify with one another through a number of shared characteristics (such as culture, language, or religion).
>
> (Baker 2014, 74)[6]

Baker argues that Newfoundland[7] ethnicity exists and has developed since the 17th century, solidifying in the mid to late 1800s (2014, 82) and includes key characteristics of ethno-symbolism including (but not limited to) a collective name, historical memories, a specific homeland and a sense of solidarity for large parts of the population (2014, 86).

Harter (2004) also notes that generations of sealing and the working-class experiences with the sealing industry greatly inform the fostering and articulation of the thoughts, beliefs, values and customs that we now identify as distinct to Newfoundlanders and Labradorians. Furthermore, the socio-linguistic distinctiveness of Newfoundland (and Labrador) English is yet another aspect of Newfoundland and Labrador's distinctiveness that identifies Newfoundlanders and Labradorians as a cultural and ethnic group separate from Canadians (Clarke 2012; also see Smith 2017). Therefore, when protesters came into Newfoundland and Labrador, starting in the 1960s, distinguishing between local peoples and non-locals was very easy to do. The ethnic and cultural characteristics of Newfoundlanders and Labradorians made locals easily identifiable targets, with their identifiability amplified by their inability to move their cultural practices, like seal hunting and associated activities elsewhere away from protesters, and still exist as a cohesive, active cultural group.[8]

In 1969 when IFAW started the formalized anti-sealing movement (IFAW n.d.; also see Davies 1970; Patey 1990), for example, Newfoundland and Labrador had only been part of Canada for 20 years (Burke 2021c).[9] Canadian, and international, protesters from organizations like Greenpeace (initially from British Columbia) (Greenpeace n.d.), began to protest against Newfoundland and Labrador's sealing; they argued that sealing is not an acceptable practice (e.g. Weyler 2004; Patey 1990; IFAW 2019). The cultural distinctiveness of sealers in Newfoundland and Labrador, especially rural residents in many centuries-old traditional coastal communities in the province, was ignored and dismissed as antiquated. The actions, attitudes and behaviours of anti-sealing protesters who came overwhelmingly from outside of the province conveyed a desire to get sealers and their families to assimilate into an idea of what protesters viewed as "Canadian", whether locals wanted to change or not, at the expense of their own Newfoundlander and Labradorian identities, traditions and cultural practices (Burke 2021c).

Cultural violence is in effect "an invariant, a 'permanence'" (Galtung 1990, 295) and the aim of assimilation underpinning the anti-sealing messaging was so prevalent in the 1970s and 1980s that even school children in Newfoundland and Labrador understood what was happening around them and were upset and frustrated by it. For example, in 1977 an observer report on the seal hunt noted that during a presentation and discussion with fisheries officers, Newfoundland school children in the Northern Peninsula were distressed by the actions and attitudes of the protesters and their Canadian supporters.

> It was obvious that the students and their teachers were upset at the attitudes of others Canadians, who failed to understand the manner in which they lived, their emphasis on family life and not on money. Their desire is to live their own lives in the manner in which they have been living for many generations, a life style which continues to be a driving force in the outports of Newfoundland. They believed that others in Canada were attempting to force them to give up their way of live to adopt that of those in the mainland. This was unacceptable to them. They were frustrated by the lack of understanding of their geographic difference, their social and cultural life and their opportunities for employment peculiar to the Newfoundlander.
>
> (Roswell 1977, 24)

Local people struggled under the unrelenting pressure from activists and media that portrayed their culture as backward. Even local children knew that protesters viewed them as "needing re-education into the 'Canadian' way of doing things" (Burke 2021b; also see Burke 2021c).

Again in 1985 Newfoundland school children sought cultural tolerance and understanding about their ethnicity and the role of sealing in their culture as they observed their family members and communities being abused by protesters that dismissed their right to exist. Students at a rural school on the Northern Peninsula wrote:

> We ... believe that the seal hunt is a vital part of our economical, social and cultural life; therefore we are writing this brief to express our concern. Attacks have been made on our culture before, but never more so than the ever-present frenzy being displayed by various protest groups. The seal hunt has been a vital part of the Newfoundland fishery for hundreds of years and has been a reliable source of income during the long, harsh winter months.
>
> (Royal Commission on Seals and Sealing Industry in Canada 1985)

The experiences of cultural violence reported by school children in Newfoundland in 1985 are serious, and yet largely ignored in historical and contemporary discussions about the legacy and outcomes of the anti-sealing movement. A plausible reason why the experiences of children, in particular, might have become ignored by protesters and debates about the merits of sealing – commercial or otherwise – might be linked to the repercussions of cultural violence which "preaches, teaches, admonishes, eggs on, and dulls us into seeing exploitation and/or repression as normal and natural, or into not seeing them...at all" (Galtung 1990, 296).

While local sealers and their families in Newfoundland and Labrador understood their cultural distinctiveness from those attacking them made them targets, decades of repetitive narratives aimed to stigmatize sealing and sealers have dulled audiences (e.g. media, national and international politicians and protesters) to recognizing, acknowledging and caring about the harm that rural and coastal peoples in Newfoundland and Labrador have been experiencing. Instead, the effort to undermine the sealing dimension and heritage of Newfoundland and Labrador culture is seemingly rooted in the belief of some of the more aggressive and vocal protesters that they were ultimately educating Newfoundlanders and Labradorians into the correct way of being Canadian, which in their view means not sealing.[10]

Unidirectional Violence and Immobility of Targets

The concept of unidirectional violence – one group attacking another unprovoked – is controversial to apply in protracted disputes, like the anti-sealing protests. Many high-profile protesting organizations like Greenpeace and Sea Shepherd have argued, for example, that their work is grounded in the philosophy of non-violence (e.g. Greenpeace Canada 2022; Greenpeace UK n.d.;

Sea Shepherd n.d.). However, again reflecting on Johan Galtung's work on cultural violence (1990, 293), one side's perception of their self-defined non-violence does not necessarily mean that their attitudes, actions and behaviours which they frame as non-violent are in fact non-violent from the perspective of those on the receiving end of the strategies and tactics employed (e.g. see Goodin 1992).[11] Furthermore, instigators of violence may point to actions by those they target who respond in ways that may also be interpreted as violent which can lead to a cycle of attitudes, actions and behaviours on both sides that may escalate a situation.

For example, Sea Shepherd protestor Jerry Vlasak allegedly received a bloody nose after purportedly being hit in the face by a Newfoundland sealer on the ice while participating in anti-sealing protests in 2005. During the altercation Sea Shepherd claims that "8 sealers physically assaulted 7 Sea Shepherd crewmembers on the ice with hak-a-piks and clubs" (Sea Shepherd 2005). However, if we look at this situation from the perspective of the sealers on the ice, Vlasak came to Canada to participate in Sea Shepherd's direct action, which it frames as non-violent, with a likely outcome of the direct action being physical interference in seal hunting activities.

Additionally Vlasak also reportedly promoted the idea that the assassination of hunters to protect animals is a valid way to protect animals (Doward 2004). If we consider what the atmosphere would have been like on the ice for the sealers leading up to and during the confrontation with Sea Shepherd protesters, the sealers would likely have learned that an individual protesting against them on the ice for Sea Shepherd is reportedly endorsing assassination and this would have likely contributed to an atmosphere of fear and anxiety when the protesters and sealers met (e.g. Standing Committee on Fisheries and Oceans 2006; CBC 2005a, b). Underscoring the seriousness of Vlasak's position, the year before his sealing protests he was supposedly banned from entering the United Kingdom in 2004 because he promoted the killing of scientists to protect animals (Doward 2004).

Therefore, this book argues that a case can be made that the decades of anti-sealing activism against Newfoundlanders and Labradorians qualifies as unidirectional violence because in the sealing campaigns Newfoundlanders and Labradorians are almost always in the responding self-defence position. Over the decades protesters have come into rural and isolated communities and coastal areas in or near Newfoundland and Labrador without local invitation or desire. The experience of communities in the 1970s–early 1980s in particular, such as St. Anthony on the Northern Peninsula, was akin to siege warfare; the small rural community and local sealers from the area were inundated with protesters and media for the months of the seal hunt (March–May), year after year in their community and while on the ice with no means to make the situation stop (Patey 1990). The only possible "out" for locals to get protesters to leave them alone would have been to abandon hundreds of years, and thousands of years for Indigenous Newfoundlanders and Labradorians, of sealing practices and the cultural, economic and other benefits associated with it.

The intentional and explicit attribution of conduct/tribal stigma (Page 1984, 11; Goffman 1963) is a key way in which protesters targeted sealing and pushed people into abandoning cultural and economic practices and discouraged the passing on of local traditional sealing knowledge. Protesters promoted the devaluation of the rights and experiences of sealers and their culture by presenting themselves as moral authorities who are social agents for positive change and locals as cruel, uncivilized savages that need to be educated and corrected.[12] As social agents, protesters and organizations in effect sought to "impose their vision of the world or the vision of their own position in that world, and [seek] to define their social identity" (Bourdieu 1987, 10–11). In this instance, protesters have in effect argued that sealing is antithetical to what it meant to be a good Canadian and/or global citizen. In doing so activists actively stigmatized sealers as part of their process to push for change because audiences confer stigmatization "to expose something unusual and bad about the moral status of the signifier" (Goffman 1963, 1)

To pursue their agendas for change, protesters created situations in which the outcomes could be used to portray sealers as the savages and barbarians they need them to be to argue the moral legitimacy of their actions and justify dehumanizing sealers and their cultural practices. For example, in 1977 when Paul Watson lead Greenpeace members on the ice during the annual seal hunt, Greenpeace members are reported to have proceeded to bully, intimidate, destroy property and, in at least one instance, take a sealer hostage on the ice by surrounding him and stopping him from moving while shouting insults and abuse (Rowsell 1977; Burke 2021c). One official observer to the 1977 hunt also recalled that Watson instigated a direct action stunt where he hooked himself to a load of seal pelts being brought onboard a vessel by a winch. The winch operator did not see Watson and mistakenly dropped him into icy water. Once the mistake was realized, sealers from the vessel rescued Watson. Watson claimed he was paralyzed, so the sealers took him aboard their vessel to try and help him but once he was onboard and they got him dry, Watson began to walk around the vessel, clearly not paralyzed, and taunted the sealers with threats of legal action (Rowsell 1977, 23). In Watson's view, however, he stands by his belief that his actions while protesting sealing are examples of non-violent intervention (Essemlali and Watson 2013; also see Weyler 2004).

Again in 1977, Greenpeace members reportedly destroyed sealers' equipment by throwing it, and harvested pelts, into the water (Patey 1990). At one point four Greenpeace members were observed to have taken a sealer hostage, isolating the sealer on a moving piece of ice in March 1977.

Four of them [Greenpeace members] surrounded a sealer and refused to let him move from the pan. This intimidation can only be considered as bullying. In spite of the intimidation, the harassment and the provocation, the Newfoundland sealer did not strike out against Greenpeace members or attempt to take any form of defensive action.

(Roswell 1977, 25)

On top of the risks of physical violence, sealers and their families have been repeatedly subjected to psychological terrorizing through highly derogatory, often anonymous, letters, emails and telephone calls, and the weaponization of familial love through threats to kidnap, torture and murder the children and grandchildren of sealers.

For example, in the 2005 documentary *My Ancestors Were Rogues and Murderers* an anti-sealing protester was recorded contacting a sealer by telephone, saying:

Would you like a meat hook stuck in your brain? Lay off the animal rights people. I think it's fucking reprehensible. You people out there, you don't even know whose money you're living off of. You're living off of Central Canada and Western Canada. You can't even make your own fucking way in life. If you don't like it get the fuck out of our country you fucking assholes.

(Troake 2005)

Many individuals received messages filled with threats and bigotry, such as the one above which tells Newfoundland sealers to conform to the "Canadian" way of being or leave the country.

In 2006, for example, while testifying for the Canadian Standing Committee on Fisheries and Oceans, sealing advocate James Winter recalled "I've had death threats. I've had people threatening to skin my children alive, when they were much younger, so that I would understand how a mommy seal feels" (Standing Committee on Fisheries and Oceans 2006). Others, like John Gillett, a fisherman from Twillingate, Newfoundland, have tried desperately to keep local traditional sealing knowledge and practices alive for current and future generations but is in despair as their culture erodes around them: "I killed my first seal when I was only 12 years old, and sold pelts in 1980s when the price was only a dollar to try to keep the industry going. Now it's being taken away from me bit by bit" (Standing Committee on Fisheries and Oceans 2006).

John Gillet is not alone in his concern that the decades of anti-sealing protests are destroying the Newfoundland and Labrador culture. Hedley Butler, a fisherman and a town councillor for the community of Bonavista, Newfoundland, expressed anxiety about the impact of anti-sealing movement: "The seal fishery for fishermen in coastal communities is a very important part of our livelihood. We have taken seals for the past 500 years for food and as a means of making a living. [But now we] have thousands of people in our communities who are leaving" (Standing Committee on Fisheries and Oceans 2006).

There is a profound sense of defeat and sadness amongst fishers who are sealers as they experience decades of degradation and dismissal of their experience by people with the ability to help. The frustration is perhaps most eloquently summarized by fisher/sealer Garry Troake:

> I'm fed up with incompetent politicians. I am tired of rich movie stars and the like that know as much about seals as I know about being Captain Kirk. I'm sick of animal welfare groups who are about as concerns about the future of seals as I am about the insects that live in the firewood in my basement. I am fed up with hypocritical scientists and misinformed, sensationalised media coverage and I'm angered with some sealers that treat our resource like it's so much garbage. Why can't common sense prevail? ... As a sealer, I don't think I'm asking for much. Just some good scientific advice, good government management, good accurate media coverage and maybe a true environmental group that will realize that you won't save the seals by destroying what I do any more than you'll save the rainforest by destroying the native peoples.
>
> (Troake 2005)

Individuals who have been strong believers in Newfoundland and Labrador's culture, such as the late Garry Troake,[13] attempted to defend the way of life of sealers and on multiple occasions protesters spat in his face. On one occasion: "A young woman spat in Garry's face at a seal protest, and all Garry did was wipe the spit away with his sleeve, look at her, and smile. This put her over the edge, with her swearing and stamping her feet" (Gillett 2015, 65–6).

As the years progress, however, fear of protesters and their violence has sapped many sealers and their communities of their ability to hold out against the desire of outsiders to eradicate their cultural and economic practices. Many people now self-censor and discourage younger generations from participating in or talking about sealing to avoid protester violence, which coupled with mass outmigration (Government of Newfoundland and Labrador 2020) is corroding Newfoundland and Labrador's traditional sealing practices as some community elders/elderly and practitioners who hold the traditional sealing knowledge fear of openly discussing sealing and passing on knowledge and traditions to the youth that are still around.

As targets of protesters, actively participating members of traditional sealing cultures in Canada are effectively immobile. Their continuation depends on their presence in, and access to, their coastal communities and coastlines. They cannot continue their existence as cohesive, active cultural groups by moving elsewhere because they depend on unimpeded access to, and the presence of, the seal herds during the stages of its seasonal migration cycle. This means that sealing cultures in the Canadian Arctic and Northeast are tied to their particular geographic areas along the Canadian coastline where their cultures are located, formed and evolved, meaning they cannot move away from their returning attackers in search of refuge and also continue to exist at the same time.

Notes

1 It is important to acknowledge that, to the best of this author's knowledge, Moore continues to be against commercial sealing and is proud of his work against the seal hunt, and his comments quoted in this book were not made in the context of the sealing debate but rather a reflection on the state of the environmental movement as a whole.

2 Acknowledgement of Indigenous peoples in the sealing debate and more nuanced discourse around Indigenous traditional rights, for example, only started to get some traction in the mid-1980s (Woods 1986).

3 According to Wright, the anti-sealing protests "is a direct intrusion of *them* against *us*, of urban values clashing with rural traditions, which seems to sum up various complaints Newfoundlanders [and Labradorians] have about the intrusion of mainland cultural values to the detriment of their own heritage" (Wright 1981, 62).

4 Broadly speaking culture is made up of learned behaviours and attitudes (thoughts, beliefs, values and customs) and ethnicity is based around identifying with those that you have strong commonality, especially in areas such as culture, a common language/dialect and ancestry (it can be from the same racial group like people who identify as ethnically Indian or Chinese, but ancestry can also be people who identify from the same city/region such as Sicily or from a broader geographic area like the British Isles or Scandinavia).

5 Similar arguments of cultural and ethnic distinctiveness can be made for the coastal Quebecois of the Quebec North Shore and Magdalen Islands who also have strong "elements of common culture" associated with sealing and recognition in Canada as distinct people; Quebec is recognized as a nation within a nation in Canada (Secrétariat du Québec aux relations canadiennes 2015).

6 Baker (2014, 79) goes on to assert that the origins of a Newfoundland ethnicity date back to the 17th century: "The hybrid nature of seventeenth century Newfoundland society – that is, the intertwined resident and migratory fishery – perhaps heralded the beginning of a Newfoundland ethnogenesis. This is especially true as the Newfoundland settlers began to accumulate the markers of a Newfoundland ethnicity not only through interaction with their physical environment but also through emergent cultural integration and religious tolerance".

7 The official name of Newfoundland and Labrador was the Dominion of Newfoundland at the point of Confederation with Canada in 1949, though Labrador was long-known as Labrador beyond the official name of the country, later province. Given that Baker's assessment of the emergence of a Newfoundland post-Confederation "ethnicity", using Confederation as the analytical starting point, this may explain why Labrador is not overtly discussed in the analysis as it may be implicitly included as part of the dominion/province's ethnicity which at that time was legally referred to as the Province of Newfoundland in the post-Confederation period.

8 Examples of activities include social gatherings around the processing and sharing of seal meat, consuming seal meat they hunted at home and in social places like community halls and making and wearing clothes and other items with seal furs that are socially acceptable to wear without fear of appraisal or physical attack.

9   Before joining Canada, Newfoundland and Labrador was a separate, older country from Canada within the British Empire. Newfoundland and Labrador's amalgamation into Canada includes a complicated journey of questionable actions taken by the Canadian and British governments that caused tensions and mistrust in the Canada-Newfoundland and Labrador bilateral relations that continue to fester to this day (e.g. Baker 2003; Cadigan 2006). For example, in 1944, during bilateral discussions about Confederation: "Canadian interest would also be prompted by the economic potential of Labrador's resources, especially its potential iron ore reserves in western Labrador [present day Labrador City and Wabush area] which Canadian government officials were aware of by 1944. Canada in 1947 would keep knowledge of its discovery by a Canadian company secret so Newfoundlanders [and Labradorians] would not be adversely influenced in their perception of Canada" (Baker 2003, 38–9). Both at the time, and in retrospect, there are Newfoundlanders and Labradorians who "felt [and continue to feel] coerced into Confederation not only by overt British interests and Canadian lust for its resources, but, many suspected, by covert manipulation of the narrowly decisive 1948 referendum" (Lowenthal 2017, 156; also see Malone 2012, 239). There were two referendums about whether the Dominion of Newfoundland, as Newfoundland and Labrador was then known, would join Canada. The first referendum did not result in a vote to join Canada but a second vote was held in 1948 and the Dominion voted to become a Canadian province by a margin of 7000 votes: "On July 22, 1948, the option to join Canada won by the narrow margin of 7,000 votes – 52% voting for confederation with Canada and 47% for responsible government. (The count was protested by the losing side for a generation) … In the newest province of Canada, black drapes were hung in mourning. Black flags were raised in a mute elegy for the lost nation" (CBC 2001).

10   An irony of promoting sealing as not a Canadian practice omits sealing traditions in other provinces in rural and coastal communities in places like Quebec, Nova Scotia and Prince Edward Island.

11   Robert Goodin's research on non-violence in environmental and animal rights activism includes an exploration of violence-prone environmentalists, such as "the self-styled 'monkeywrenchers' of the American West". Goodin argues that these activists claim their work is non-violent resistance because their activities are "not directed towards harming human beings or other forms of life" but rather "inanimate machines and tools". The monkeywrenchers use tactics like spiking roads and trees and unscrewing crucial bolts in machinery and argue that this is non-violent, but Goodin points out that these activities can cause enormous harm to sawyers and millers such as causing major economic harm to businesses and potentially life threatening and altering injuries to workers due to machinery malfunctions or hitting a spike in a tree while sawing it, for example (Goodin 1992, 134).

12   According to Nuttall (1990, 240), there is also a tendency to describe Inuit subsistence as traditional but this is problematic because "the definition of tradition is tenuous, invoking images of a romantic idealised past, before the days of European contact, when both humans and animals were perceived to be part of an integrated biological harmony".

13   Troake and his colleague Roger Blake lost their lives in a commercial fishing accident in 2000 (Gillett 2015, 65–6).

Conclusion

To date the mainstream international discussion about sealing has largely focused on the narratives and agendas advocated by environmental and animal rights groups with messaging about the morality and cruelty of hunting dominating public discourse and awareness. The focus has muddled the public's understanding of the topic with simplistic emotive narratives, competing and contradictory messages and the deliberate devaluation of the experiences of the peoples that are paying the real costs – physically, culturally, psychologically and economically – for what the campaigners are doing.

This book injects more nuance into the sealing debate by exploring the underrepresented perceptive of the ground-zero targets of the campaigning because their experiences remain largely ignored and over-simplistically presented by cultural outsiders. It accomplished this by providing a critical exploration of the discursive gap that downplays consideration of asymmetrical conflicts and experiences of cultural violence where activist organizations are the more powerful actors and are the aggressors against vulnerable targets. Specifically through approaching the anti-sealing debate using the literature on cultural violence, stigma and moral legitimacy, this book seeks to bring the perspective of sealers, their families and communities to the forefront, using the case of Newfoundland and Labrador. It highlights the insidiousness of cultural violence, when experiences of violence are normalized in wider society to the point that few can be bothered to acknowledge and openly call out questionable campaigning legacies, strategies, tactics, and actions, attitudes and behaviours they have encouraged, such as sieging isolated communities, promotion of cultural assimilation and threats to harm children.

The book highlights the fact that inflictors of cultural violence are not solely states and state-supporters actors. Through their actions, attitudes and behaviours, environmental and animal rights organizations can also conduct themselves and seek to realize their agendas in ways that contribute to, and cause, experiences of cultural violence. Despite Greenpeace often being conflated with the anti-sealing cause due to its early high-profile campaigning in the 1970s and early 1980s, it must be noted that no one environmental and animal rights organization bears sole responsibility for the cultural violence experienced by rural and coastal fishers/sealers, their families and communities in Newfoundland and Labrador. This point is not to absolve any specific organization for their part in the outcomes they encouraged, participated in and helped bring about, perhaps most startlingly the emboldening of activists and protesters to anonymously threaten sealers and their families with the torture and murder of their children in Newfoundland and Labrador. Rather the point is to acknowledge that there are many activist fingers in the anti-sealing pie, so to speak.

Over the decades it took the willingness of organizations, their members and supporters to normalize harm and dehumanize people who opposed them to bring about the cultural violence illustrated in this book. However, after decades of anti-sealing campaigns, some organizations have benefited and contributed more to the anti-sealing cause and for longer, and therefore arguably have more responsibility to bear for outcomes resulting from their advocacy.

We should also acknowledge that experiences of cultural violence in the sealing debate against ethnic and cultural groups that are not explicitly and exclusively Indigenous do have negative implications for Indigenous sealing interests and self-determination. The book broadly outlines the Newfoundland and Labrador cultural violence experiences and the knock-on effect it broadly has on Indigenous interests in Canada by noting the attempts to artificially and externally impose a moral cultural hierarchy in the sealing debate. Activists, many of whom classify sealing as a cruel slaughter, interject a seemingly arbitrary racial and ethnic exceptionalism that elevates the killing of a seal by an Inuit/Indigenous hunter as justified but reprehensible murder conducted by a non-Indigenous hunter. As the book discusses, by creating a moral grey zone on which people are permissible to seal hunt and in what manner, activists have pigeon-holed Indigenous peoples into a narrow frame of acceptable sealing practices and benefit parameters that effectively dictate to them about how they are permitted to use renewal natural resources within their own homelands. By simultaneously stigmatizing alternative subsistence sealing cultural practices and commercial activities, activists reinforce a moralistic cage around sealing by Indigenous nations by setting artificial boundaries to inhibit Indigenous peoples through public narratives and creative messaging campaigns which impose inconsistent determinations of acceptability in the human–seal coexistence.

Lastly, the book challenges the idea that only a narrow understanding of cultural rights and experiences warrant consideration by activists, governments and academics/researchers when discussing policy-making that affects seal hunting. The lack of adequate acknowledgement and exploration of the argument that cultural violence underpins much of the anti-sealing campaigning dismisses the negative impact that activists have had on the social and cultural fabric of many Indigenous and non-Indigenous peoples throughout rural and coastal fishing communities in Canada and in the Circumpolar North. Furthermore, by not acknowledging the cultural violence experienced by sealers in places like Newfoundland and Labrador, activists, academics and policy-makers are stunting efforts of Inuit and other Indigenous activists and leadership and their work challenging seal product bans which limit their ability to develop their economies in sustainable and renewal ways.

To acknowledge the cultural violence inflicted on sealers means having to reflect on harsh questions that many would perhaps like ignored or dismissed, such as should the EU seal product ban, which is based on a moral objection, be re-evaluated? Why are organizations against sealing not openly condemning protesters and activists who use anonymous threats to murder children as a pressure tactic against sealers and their families? And why are activists and European policy-makers dictating to Inuit and Indigenous peoples about under what conditions their killing of a seal is considered morally acceptable? As it stands, the normalization of cultural violence against non-explicitly Indigenous sealing cultures like Newfoundland and Labrador creates much local distress and harm, while simultaneously boxing in Inuit and Indigenous peoples so as to limit their abilities to use traditional knowledge, practices and renewable resources in their homelands to grow their economies.

References

Allen, Jeremiah. (1979). "Anti-Sealing as an Industry." *Journal of Political Economy* 87: 423–8.

Baker, James. (2014). "A Newfoundland Ethnicity? The Political Implications of Post-Confederation Nationalism in Newfoundland." *Studies in Ethnicity and Nationalism* 14: 74–100.

Baker, Melvin. (2003). "Falling into the Canadian Lap: The Confederation of Newfoundland and Canada 1945–1949." *Royal Commission on Renewing and Strengthening Our Place in Canada.* https://www.gov.nl.ca/publicat/royalcomm/research/fallingintothecanadianlap.pdf.

Baldoli, R. and Radaelu, C.M. (2019). "What Has Nonviolence Got to do with the EU?" *Journal of Common Market Studies* 57(5): 1165–81.

Baron, D.P. (2001). "Private Politics, Corporate Social Responsibility, and Integrated Strategy." *Journal of Economics and Management Strategy* 10: 7–45.

Baur, D. and Palazzo, G. (2011). "The Moral Legitimacy of NGOs as Partners of Corporations." *Business Ethics Quarterly* 21: 579–604.

Belsky, Leora and Klagsbrun, Rachel. (2018). "The Return of Cultural Genocide?" *The European Journal of International Law* 29: 373–96.

Benoit First Nation. (2016). "Visiting With Our Mi'kmaq Elders: Cape St. George, Newfoundland." https://www.benoitfirstnation.ca/elder_book_index.html.

Berster, Lars. (2015). "The Alleged non-existence of Cultural Genocide." *Journal of International Criminal Justice* 13: 677–92.

Betsill, Michele M. and Corell, Elisabeth. (2007). "NGO Diplomacy: The Influence of Nongovernmental Organizations." In *International Environmental Negotiations,* edited by Corell E. and Betsill, M.M. MIT Press.

Boldorn, A. and Major, B. (2016). "Stigma." In *The SAGE Encyclopedia of Theory in Psychology,* edited by H.L. Miller. Thousand Oaks: SAGE.

Bourdieu, P. (1987). "What Makes a Social Class? On the Theoretical and Practical Existence of Groups." *Berkeley Journal of Sociology* 32: 1–18.

Brown, Cassie and Horwood, Harold. (1972). *Death on the Ice: The Great Newfoundland Sealing Disaster of 1914.* Anchor Canada: Penguin Random House.

Burgwald, Jon. (2016). "Where Does Greenpeace Stand on Seal Hunting?" *Greenpeace,* 21 January. https://www.greenpeace.org/canada/en/story/424/where-does-greenpeace-stand-on-seal-hunting/.

Burke, Danita Catherine. (2018). *International Disputes and Cultural Ideas in the Canadian Arctic.* London: Palgrave Macmillan.

Burke, Danita Catherine. (2020). "Re-establishing Legitimacy After Stigmatization: Greenpeace in the North American North." *Polar Record* 56(e26): 1–12.

Burke, D.C. (2021a) "Case for a Newfoundland and Labrador Northern Strategy." *The Polar Journal* 11(2): 381–392.

Burke, Danita Catherine. (2021b). "How Europe's Ban on Seal Products Turned Frontier Communities into Pariahs." *The Conversation*, September 2. https://theconversation.com/how-europes-ban-on-seal-products-turned-frontier-communities-into-pariahs-161730.

Burke, Danita Catherine. (2021c). "The Case for a Greenpeace Apology to Newfoundland and Labrador." *The Northern Review* 51: 173–87.

Burke, Danita Catherine. (2021d). "The Relationship between Kanngiqtugaapik/Clyde River and Greenpeace: An Interview with Mayor Jerry Natanine." *Arctic* 74(1): 106–10.

Burke, Danita Catherine. (2022a). "Reflecting on the Seal Hunt and the Anti-Sealing Movement – A Conversation with former President of the Canadian Sealers Association James Winter." *Women in the Arctic and Antarctic*, May 31. https://womeninthearcticandantarctic.com.

Burke, Danita Catherine. (2022b). "Navigating a Research Topic that is Close to Home." *Arctic* 75(3): 393–5.

Burke, Danita Catherine. (2023). "An Interview with Documentary Filmmaker Anne Troake: Reflecting on Anti-sealing Activism and its Impact on Rural Coastal Peoples in Canada." *Arctic* 76: 107–10.

Butterworth, Andrew and Richardson, Mary. (2013). "A Review of Animal Welfare Implications of the Canadian Commercial Seal Hunt." *Marine Policy* 38(1): 457–69.

Cadigan, Sean T. (2006). "Regional Politics are Class Politics: A Newfoundland and Labrador Perspective on Regions." *Acadiensis* 35: 163–8.

Cadigan, Sean T. (2013). *Death on Two Fronts: National Tragedies and the Fate of Democracy in Newfoundland, 1914–34.* Canada: Penguin.

Campbell, Bradley. (2009). "Genocide as Social Control." *Sociological Theory* 27: 150–72.

Causadias, José M. (2020). "What is culture? Systems of people, places, and Practices." *Applied Developmental Science* 24: 310–22.

CBC. (2001). "Newfoundland Decides its Future." Canada: A People's History. https://www.cbc.ca/history/EPISCONTENTSE1EP15CH2PA1LE.html.

CBC News. (2005a). "Watson Defends Controversial Board Member." April 20. https://www.cbc.ca/news/canada/newfoundland-labrador/watson-defends-controversial-board-member-1.558370.

CBC News. (2005b). "Vlasak's Views Not Supported: Sea Shepherd." April 21. https://www.cbc.ca/news/canada/newfoundland-labrador/vlasak-s-views-not-supported-sea-shepherd-1.542100.

CBC News. (2009). "FAQs: The Atlantic Seal Hunt." May 5. https://www.cbc.ca/news/canada/faqs-the-atlantic-seal-hunt-1.803159.

CBC News. (2017). "PETA's Anti-commercial Sealing Videos "Devastating" to Inuit, Critic Says." April 21. https://www.cbc.ca/news/canada/north/peta-anti-commercial-sealing-inuk-critic-1.4078713.

CBC Radio. (1965). "New Rules to Protect Seals." April 2. https://www.cbc.ca/archives/entry/new-rules-to-protect-seals.

CBC The Broadcast with Jane Adey. (2021). "Sealer Reacts to Call for Greenpeace to Apologize to Sealers in NL." *CBC Radio*, June 2. https://www.cbc.ca/listen/live-radio/1-122-the-broadcast/clip/15847237-sealer-reacts-call-greenpeace-apologize-sealers-n.l.

Clarke, Sandra. (2012). "Phonetic change in Newfoundland English." *World Englishes* 31: 503–18.

Cochrane, J.A. and Parsons, A.W. (1949). *The Story of Newfoundland*. Toronto: Ginn and Company.

Collingwood, V. (2006). "Non-governmental Organisations, Power and Legitimacy in International Society." *Review of International Studies* 32: 439–54.

Connor, D.P. (2014). "Stigma and Stigma Management." In *Encyclopedia of Social Deviance*, edited by C.J. Forsyth and H. Copes. Thousands Oaks: SAGE Publications, Inc.

Crocker, J., Major, B.N. and Steele, C. (1998). "Social Stigma." In *Handbook of Social Psychology*, edited by S. Fiske, D. Gilbert and G. Lindzey. Boston: McGraw-Hill.

Crockett, Zachary. (2015). "The Business of Seal Clubbing." *Priceonomics*, September 1. https://priceonomics.com/the-business-of-seal-clubbing/.

Dale, Norman and Mills, Hal. (1979). "Coastal Water Boundaries: Issues and Jurisdictions." *Canadian Water Resources Journal* 4(3): 35–45.

Daubanes, Julien Xavier and Rochet, Jean Charles. (2016). "A Theory of NGO Activism." MIT Center for Energy and Environmental Policy Research. https://www.researchgate.net/publication/307875390_A_Theory_of_NGO_Activism.

Dauvergne, P. and Neville, K.J. (2011). "Mindbombs of Right and Wrong: Cycles of Contention in the Activist Campaign to Stop Canada's Seal Hunt." *Environmental Politics* 20(2): 192–209.

Davies, Brian. (1970). *Savage Luxury: The Slaughter of the Baby Seals*. London: Souvenir Press.

Dawson, Joanna. (2014). "Newfoundland's 1914 Sealing Disaster." *Canada's History*, March 31, 2014. https://www.canadashistory.ca/explore/environment/newfoundland-s-1914-sealing-disaster.

Department of Fisheries and Aquaculture. (2012a). *Key Messages and Facts on Canada's Sealing Industry*. Government of Newfoundland and Labrador. St. John's, Newfoundland and Labrador, Canada.

Department of Fisheries and Aquaculture. (2012b). *Commercial Utilization*. Government of Newfoundland and Labrador.

Department of Fisheries and Aquaculture. (2012c). *Industry Background*. Government of Newfoundland and Labrador.

Dhanani, Alpa and Connolly, Ciaran. (2015). "Non-governmental Organizational Accountability: Talking the Talk and Walking the Walk?" *Journal of Business Ethics* 129: 613–637.

Doward, Jamie. (2004). "Kill Scientists, Says Animal Rights Chief." *The Guardian*, July 25. https://www.theguardian.com/society/2004/jul/25/health.animalrights.

Elliot-Meisel, E. (1998). *Arctic Diplomacy: Canada and the United States in the Northwest Passage*. New York: Peter Lang.

Ellul, J. (1965). *Propaganda: The Formation of Men's Attitudes*. Translated from French by Konrad Kellen and Jean Lerner. New York: Vintage Books.

Engel, Monica T., Jerry J. Vaske and Alistair J. Bath. (2021). "Seal Hunting in Newfoundland from the Perspective of Local People." *Marine Policy* 128(2021): 1–8.

Essemlali, Lamya and Watson, Paul. (2013). *Captain Paul Watson: Interview with a Pirate*. Richmond Hill: Firefly Books Ltd.

European Commission. (2016). "WTO Cases: Cases Involving the EU." WT/DS400 - European Communities - Measures Prohibiting the Importation and Marketing of Seal Products. https://trade.ec.europa.eu/wtodispute/show.cfm?id=475&code=2.

European Commission. (2019a). "Trade in Seal Products: Legislative History of the File." https://ec.europa.eu/environment/biodiversity/animal_welfare/seals/history.htm.

European Commission. (2019b). "Trade in Seal Products: Scope of the EU Seal Ban." https://ec.europa.eu/environment/biodiversity/animal_welfare/seals/seal_hunting.htm.

European Commission. (2020). "Report from the Commission to the European Parliament and the Council: On the implementation of Regulation (EC) 1007/2009, as amended by Regulation (EU) 2015/1775, on the Trade in Seal Products." Brussels. Available from: https://eur-lex.europa.eu/legal-content/en/TXT/?uri=CELEX:52020DC0004.

Farquhar, Samantha. (2020). "Inuit Seal Hunting in Canada: Emerging Narratives in an Old Controversy." *Arctic* 73(1): 13–9.

Felsberg, Susan. (1985). "A Brief to the Royal Commission on Seals and the Sealing Industry in Canada." Centre for Newfoundland Studies, Queen Elizabeth 2 Library, Memorial University of Newfoundland. St. John's, Newfoundland and Labrador, Canada. File SH362.R7v.102.

Fisheries and Oceans Canada. (1979). "Historical and Sociological Perspective of Sealing: History of Sealing." Centre for Newfoundland Studies, Queen Elizabeth 2 Library, Memorial University of Newfoundland. St. John's, Newfoundland and Labrador, Canada. File SH363 .S39 1979.

Fisheries and Oceans Canada. (1996). "Chapter Six: Seal Licensing Policy for Eastern Canada." July 1. https://www.dfo-mpo.gc.ca/reports-rapports/regs/licences-permis/ch6-eng.htm.

Fisheries and Oceans Canada. (2011). "2011–2015 Integrated Fisheries Management Plan for Atlantic Seals." https://www.dfo-mpo.gc.ca/fisheries-peches/seals-phoques/reports-rapports/mgtplan-planges20112015/mgtplan-planges20112015-eng.html#c3.3.

Fisheries and Oceans Canada. (2016). "Notices to Fish Harvesters: Conservation Harvesting Plan (November 2016)." https://inter-l01.dfo-mpo.gc.ca/applications/opti-opei/notice-avis-detail-eng.php?pub_id=961&todo=view&type=2&region_id=4&sub_type_id=5&species=845&area=1920.

Galtung, Johan. (1990). "Cultural Violence." *Journal of Peace Research* 27: 291–305.

Gillett, John. (2015). *Leaving for the Sea Hunt: The Life of a Swiler*. St. John's: Flanker Press Limited.

Goffman, E. (1963). *Stigma: Notes on the Management of Spoiled Identity*. Englewood Cliffs: Prentice.

Goodin, Robert. (1992). *Green Political Theory*. Cambridge: Polity Press.

Government of Newfoundland and Labrador. (n.d.). "History." https://www.fishaq.gov.nl.ca/sealing/pdf/history.pdf.

Government of Newfoundland and Labrador. (2020). "Population Projections: Demographic Overview." https://www.gov.nl.ca/fin/economics/pop-overview/.

Grant, S. (1989). Myths of the North in the Canadian Ethos. *The Northern Review* 3/4(1989): 15–41.

Greenpeace. (n.d.). "About Greenpeace." https://www.greenpeace.org.uk/about-green-peace/#:~:text=Greenpeace%20was%20founded%20in%201971,was%20called%20%20%E2%80%9CThe%20Greenpeace%E2%80%9D.

Greenpeace. (1977). "Brigitte Bardot in Canada." https://www.media.greenpeace.org/archive/Brigitte-Bardot-in-Canada-27MZIF2L0KOZ.html.

Greenpeace Canada. (2022). "Protesting Peacefully, to Change the World." https://www.greenpeace.org/canada/en/about-us/protesting-peacefully-to-change-the-world/.

Greenpeace Chronicles. (1976). "Shepard's of the Labrador Front." *Greenpeace Chronicles* 2(Spring/Summer): 6.

Greenpeace Foundation. (1977). "The Canadian Seal Hunt." Centre for Newfoundland Studies, Queen Elizabeth 2 Library, Memorial University of Newfoundland. St. John's, Newfoundland and Labrador, Canada. File SH363.G711977.

Greenpeace International. (2018). "Model Code of Conduct." https://drive.google.com/file/d/18BvOe-2hIuRAfNvKNX5nuOnxIPwzONKj/view.

Greenpeace International. (2020). "Our Values." https://www.greenpeace.org/international/explore/about/values/.

Greenpeace UK. (n.d.). "How Greenpeace Creates Change." https://www.greenpeace.org.uk/about-greenpeace/how-we-create-change/.

Harter, John-Henry. (2004). "Environmental Justice for Whom? Class, New Social Movements, and the Environment: A Case Study of Greenpeace Canada, 1971–2000." *Labour/Le Travail* 54(2004): 83–119.

Hawkins, Roberta and Silver, Jennifer J. (2017). "From Selfie to #Sealfie: Nature 2.0 and the Digital Cultural Politics of an Internationally Contested Resource." *Geoforum* 79(2017): 114–23.

Hennig, Martin. (2015). "The EU Seal Products Ban: Why Ineffective Animal Welfare Protection Cannot Justify Trade Restrictions under European and International Trade Law." *Arctic Review on Law and Politics*. https://arcticreview.no/index.php/arctic/article/view/77/91#info.

Higgins, Jenny. (2013). *Perished: The 1914 Newfoundland Seal Hunt Disaster*. Boulder Publications.

Hudson, A. (2001). "NGOs' Transnational Advocacy Networks: from "Legitimacy" to "Political Responsibility"?" *Global Networks* 1(4): 331–52.

IFAW. (n.d.). "IFAW Was First Founded to End the Seal Hunt." https://www.ifaw.org/ca-en/projects/ending-the-commercial-seal-hunt-canada.

IFAW. (2019). "Our History." https://www.ifaw.org/ca-en/about/history.

IFAW. (2020). "Guiding Principles." https://www.ifaw.org/ca-en/about/guiding-principles.

Îles de la Madeleine. (2021). "Éphémérides : Un film choc tourné en 1964, Les grands phoques de la banquise." https://www.ilesdelamadeleine.com/2021/05/ephemerides-un-film-choc-tourne-en-1964-les-grands-phoques-de-la-banquise-5/.

Interim Report to the Minister of Environment from the Committee on Seals and Sealing. (1972). *Memorial University of Newfoundland, Queen Elizabeth 2nd Library*. Centre for Newfoundland Studies. File SH362 .C1754 1972.

Inuit Tapiriit Kanatami. (n.d.). "Building an Inuit Nunangat Policy Space." https://www.itk.ca/wp-content/uploads/2018/10/Inuit-Nunangat-Policy-Space-handout.pdf.

Jenkins, G.W. (2012). "Nongovernmental Organizations and the Forces Against Them: Lessons on the Anti-NGO Movement." *Brooklyn Journal of International Law* 37(2): 459–527.

Kalland, A. (2009). *Unveiling the Whale: Discourses on Whales and Whaling*. New York and Oxford: Berghahn Books.

Kashima, Emi S. (2010). "Culture and Terror Management: What is 'Culture.' in Cultural Psychology and Terror Management Theory?" *Social and Personality Psychology Compass* 4: 164–73.

Kashima, Yoshihisa. (2019). "What Is Culture For?" In *The Handbook of Culture and Psychology: Second Edition*, edited by David Matsumoto and Hyisung C. Hwang, Oxford: Oxford University Press.

Kerr, Joanna. (2014). "Greenpeace Apology to Inuit for Impacts of Seal Campaign." *Greenpeace*, June 24. https://www.greenpeace.org/canada/en/story/5473/greenpeace -apology-to-inuit-for-impacts-of-seal-campaign/.

Kingston, Lindsey. (2015). "The Destruction of Identity: Cultural Genocide and Indigenous Peoples." *Journal of Human Rights* 14: 63–83.

Lafrance, Daniele. (2017). "Canada's Seal Harvest." Economics, Resources and International Affairs Division, Library of Parliament Canada. https://lop.parl.ca/ sites/PublicWebsite/default/en_CA/ResearchPublications/201718E.

Link, Bruce G. and Phelan, Jo. (2001). "Conceptualizing Stigma." *Annual Review of Sociology* 27: 363–85.

Link, Bruce G. and Phelan, Jo. (2014). "Stigma Power." *Social Science & Medicine* 103: 24–32.

Liu, Gordon, Eng, Teck-Yong and Sekhon, Yasmin Kaur. (2014). "Managing Branding and Legitimacy: A Study of Charity Retail Sector." *Nonprofit and Voluntary Sector Quarterly* 43: 629–51.

Lowe, B. (2008). "War for the Seals: The Canadian Seal Controversy and Sociological Warfare." *Taboo: The Journal of Culture and Education* 12: 69–92.

Lowenthal, David. (2017). "Canadian Historical Nonchalance and Newfoundland Exceptionalism." *Acadiensis* 46: 152–62.

Mahoney, Kathleen. (2019). "Indigenous Legal Principles: A Reparation Path for Canada's Cultural Genocide." *American Review of Canadian Studies* 49: 207–30.

Malone, Greg. (2012). *Don't Tell the Newfoundlanders: The True Story of Newfoundland's Confederation with Canada.* Toronto: Alfred A Knopf Canada.

Marberg, A., Kranenburg, H. and Korzilius, H. (2016). "NGOs in the News: The Road to Taken-for-Grantedness." *Voluntas* 27: 2734–63.

McDermott, Dan. (1985). "Statement by Dan McDermott National Campaign Coordinator for Greenpeace Canada to the Royal Commission on Seals and the Sealing Industry in Canada." Centre for Newfoundland Studies, Queen Elizabeth 2nd Library, Memorial University of Newfoundland. St. John's, Newfoundland and Labrador, Canada. File SH362.R7v.10.

McKibbon, S. (2000). "$70,000 Video Designed Change Opinion of Seal Hunt." *Nunatsiaq News*, February 11. https://nunatsiaq.com/stories/article/70000_video _designed_change_opinion_of_seal_hunt/.

Merriam-Webster. (n.d.). "Slaughter." https://www.merriam-webster.com/dictionary/ slaughter.

Moore, Patrick. (2021). "Greenpeace's Ex-President: Is Climate Change Fake?: Patrick Moore" Interview of Patrick Moore by Chris Williamson for Modern Wisdom 373 podcast. https://www.youtube.com/watch?v=E5K5i5Wv7jQ.

Mullen, Ashley. (2020). "International Cultural Heritage Law: The Link Between Cultural Nationalism, Internationalism, and the Concept of Cultural Genocide." *Cornell Law Review* 105: 1489–526.

Murphy, J. (1916). "The Old Sealing Days." Centre for Newfoundland Studies, Queen Elizabeth 2 Library, Memorial University of Newfoundland. St. John's, Newfoundland and Labrador, Canada. File SH363.N4 M8.

Nagtzaam, Gerry, Hook, Evan van and Guilfoyle, Douglas. (2019). *International Environmental Law: A Case Study Analysis.* Ebook. Taylor & Francis.

Newfoundland and Labrador Tourism. (2021). "7 Ways in Which Newfoundland & Labrador Was First." Government of Newfoundland and Labrador. https://www.newfoundlandlabrador.com/trip-ideas/travel-stories/7-ways-in-which-newfoundland-labrador-was-first.

Novic, Elisa. (2016). *The Concept of Cultural Genocide.* Oxford: Oxford University Press.

Nunatsiaq News. (2013). "Inuit Organisation Dumps on WTO Ruling that Upholds EU Seal Product Ban." November 25. Available from: https://nunatsiaq.com/stories/article/65674inuit_org_dumps_on_wto_ruling_that_upholds_eu_seal_product_ban/.

Nuttall, Mark. (1990). "Animal Rights and Greenlandic Sealing: A Threat to Culture Survival." *Polar Record* 26(158): 240–42.

Nyyssönen, Jukka. (2022). "Frame Alignment Between Environmentalists and the Sámi in the Forest Dispute in Inari, Finland Until the 2000s: Competing Conservation Needs and Obstacles for Co-Living With the Non-Human." *Frontiers in Conservation Science* 3(925713): 1–14.

Ossewaarde, R., Nijhof, A. and Heyse, L. (2008). "Dynamics of NGO Legitimacy: How Organising Betrays Core Missions of INGOs." *Public Administration and Development* 28: 42–53.

Page, Robert. (1984). *Stigma.* London: Routledge and Kegan Paul Publisher.

Paquette, Elisabeth. (2020). "Reconciliation and Cultural Genocide: A Critique of Liberal Multicultural Strategies of Innocence." *Hypatia* 35: 143–60.

Patey, Francis. (1990). *A Battle Lost: An Unsuccessful Attempt to Save the Seal Hunt.* Grand Falls: Robinson-Blackmore Printing and Publishing Ltd.

Payam, Akhavan. (2016). "Cultural Genocide: Legal Label or Mourning Metaphor?" *McGill Law Journal* 62: 243–72.

Pescosolido, Bernice A. and Martin, Jack K. (2015). "The Stigma Complex." *Annual Review of Sociology* 41: 87–116.

PETA. (n.d.). "PETA Statement: Singer Tanya Tagaq's Support of Indigenous Seal Slaughter." https://www.peta.org/media/news-releases/peta-statement-singer-tanya-tagaqs-support-indigenous-seal-slaughter/.

PETA. (2017). "Gillian Anderson to Justin Trudeau: End the Commercial Seal Slaughter." April 27. https://www.peta.org/blog/gillian-anderson-to-justin-trudeau-end-commercial-seal-slaughter/.

Phelan, J.C., Link, B.G. and Dovidio, J.F. (2008). "Stigma and Discrimination: One Animal or Two?" *Social Science & Medicine* 67: 358–67.

Phelps Bondaroff, Teale N. and Burke, Danita Catherine. (2014). "Bridging Troubled Waters: History as Political Opportunity Structure." *Journal of Civil Society* 10(2): 165–83.

Phillips, L. (2010). "Inuit sue EU over Seal Ban." *EU Observer*, January 15. https://euobserver.com/environment/29273.

Puljek-Shank, R. (2019). "Beyond Projects: Local Legitimacy and Civil Society Advocacy in Bosnia and Herzegovina." Friedrick Ebert Stiftung. http://library.fes.de/pdf-files/bueros/sarajevo/15730-20191031.pdf.

Qalipu First Nation. (2020). "Mi'kmaq Commercial Fisheries Launches WASPU Seal Oil Capsules." October 30. http://qalipu.ca/mikmaq-commercial-fisheries-launches-waspu-seal-oil-capsules/.

Randhawa, S. (2017). "Animal Rights Activists and Inuit Clash over Canada's Indigenous Food Traditions." *The Guardian*, November 1. https://www.theguardian.com/inequality/2017/nov/01/animal-rights-activists-inuit-clash-canada-indigenous-food-traditions.

Roswell, Harry. (1977). "1977 Sealing Activities by Newfoundland Landsmen and Ships on the Front: A Report to the Committee on Seals and Sealing and The Canadian Federation of Humane Societies." Centre for Newfoundland Studies, Queen Elizabeth 2nd Library, Memorial University of Newfoundland. St. John's, Newfoundland and Labrador, Canada. File SH363.R69.

Royal Commission on Seals and Sealing Industry in Canada. (1985). "Brief to the Royal Commission on Sealing." Centre for Newfoundland Studies, Queen Elizabeth 2nd Library, Memorial University of Newfoundland. St. John's, Newfoundland and Labrador, Canada. File SH362.R7v.49.

Royal Commission on Seals and the Sealing Industry in Canada. (1986). "Volume 1: Economic Options, Prospects and Issues." Centre for Newfoundland Studies, Queen Elizabeth 2nd Library, Memorial University of Newfoundland. St. John's, Newfoundland and Labrador, Canada. File SH362.D761986.

Sanger, C.W. (1998). "Seal Fishery: Background: History, Resource and Natural Environment." Heritage Newfoundland and Labrador. https://www.heritage.nf.ca/articles/environment/sealing-fishery.php.

Scheffer, Victor B. (1984). "An Ethical View of Seals and Sealing." Testimony to the Royal Commission on Seals and the Sealing Industry in Canada. Centre for Newfoundland Studies, Queen Elizabeth 2nd Library, Memorial University of Newfoundland. St. John's, Newfoundland and Labrador, Canada. File SH362.R7v.23.

Sinclair, Peter, Hill, Robert, Lamson, Cynthia and Williamson, H.A. (1989). "Social and Cultural Aspects of Sealing in Atlantic Canada." *Report for the Royal Commission on Seals and the Sealing Industry in Canada*.

Sea Shepherd (n.d.). "General Information." https://seashepherd.org/laws-and-charters/.

Sea Shepherd. (2005). "Crew Attacked and Arrested." https://www.seashepherd.org.uk/news/archive/page-122.html.

Sea Shepherd. (2021). "Captain Paul Watson Responds to Canadian Fisheries Minister Loyola Hearn." https://www.seashepherd.org.uk/news-and-commentary/commentary/archive/captain-paul-watson-responds-to-canadian-fisheries-minister-loyola-hearn.html.

Secrétariat du Québec aux relations canadiennes. (2015). "Recognition of the Québec Nation." https://www.sqrc.gouv.qc.ca/relations-canadiennes/institutions-constitution/statut-qc/reconnaisance-nation-en.asp.

Sharp, G. (2005). *Waging Nonviolent Struggle*. Boston: Porter Sargent. https://ciaotest.cc.columbia.edu/book/ciao/0010973/f_0010973_17324.pdf.

Smith, Craig S. (2017). "Has a Canadian Slur Lost its Sting?" *The New York Times*, June 2. https://www.nytimes.com/2017/06/02/world/canada/has-a-canadian-slur-lost-its-sting.html.

Standing Committee on Fisheries and Oceans. (2006). "Tuesday, November 7, 2006." Number 022, 1st Session, 39th Parliament. House of Commons Canada. https://www.ourcommons.ca/DocumentViewer/en/39-1/FOPO/meeting-22/evidence.

Stanford, Gerald B. (1979). "Canadian Perspectives on the Future Enforcement of the Canadian Perspectives on the Future Enforcement of the Exclusive Economic

Zone: A Paper in Diplomacy and the Law of Exclusive Economic Zone: A Paper in Diplomacy and the Law of the Sea." *Dalhousie Law Journal* 5(1): 73–120.

Stone, K.H. (1954). "Human Geographic Research in the North American Northern Lands." *Arctic* 7: 321–35.

Sumner, L.W. (1983). "The Canadian Harp Seal Hunt: A Moral Assessment." *International Journal for the Study of Animal Problems* 4(2): 108–16.

The Canadian Press. (2014). "Humane Society says it Doesn't Oppose Inuit Seal Hunt." April 8. https://www.cbc.ca/news/canada/north/humane-society-says-it-doesn-t-oppose -inuit-seal-hunt-1.2603306.

The Humane Society of the United States. (2022). "About the Canadian Seal Hunt." https://www.humanesociety.org/resources/about-canadian-seal-hunt.

Thornicroft, Graham, Rose, Diana, Kassam, Aliya and Sartorium, Norman. (2007). "Stigma: Ignorance, Prejudice or Discrimination?" *British Journal of Psychiatry* 190: 192–3.

Troake, Anne. (2005). *My Ancestors Were Rogues and Murderers.* Documentary. National Film Board of Canada. https://www.nfb.ca/film/my_ancestors_were _rogues_murderers/.

Truth and Reconciliation Commission. (2015). *Honouring the Truth, Reconciling for the Future: Summary of the Final Report of the Truth and Reconciliation Commission of Canada.* The Truth and Reconciliation Commission of Canada. Ottawa, Canada.

Urbina, Ian. (2019). *The Outlaw Ocean: Journeys Across the Last Untamed Frontier.* Knopf Doubleday Publishing Group/Penguin Random House. United States.

van Krieken, Robert. (1999). "The 'Stolen Generations' and Cultural Genocide: The Forced Removal of Australian Indigenous Children from Their Families and its Implications for the Sociology of Childhood." *Childhood* 6: 297–311.

Vedder, Anton. (2007). "Questioning the Legitimacy of Non-governmental Organisations." In *NGO Involvement in International Governance and Policy: Sources of Legitimacy,* edited by Vedder, A., Collingwood, V., van Gorp, A., Kamminga, M., Logister, L., Prins, C. and Van den Bossche, P. Leiden, The Netherlands: Brill. 1–20.

Wenzel, George. (1987). "'I Was Once Independent': The Southern Seal Protest and Inuit." *Anthropologica* 29(2): 195–210.

Weyler, Rex. (2004). *Greenpeace: How a Group of Ecologists, Journalists, and Visionaries Changed the World.* Vancouver: Raincoast Books.

Wilkin, Dwane. (1998). "We're not After Inuit Seal Hunters, IFAW Claims." *Nunatsiaq News,* January 9. Available from: https://nunatsiaq.com/stories/article/were_not _after_inuit_seal_hunters_ifaw_claims/.

Woods, S.J. (1986). "The Wolf at the Door: The Anti-harvest Campaign Strikes at the Heart of North Aboriginal Economies." *Northern Perspectives* 14: 1–8.

World Trade Organization. (2014). "European Communities: Measures Prohibiting the Importation and Marketing of Seal Products." Available from: https://www.wto.org /english/tratop_e/dispu_e/400_401abr_e.pdf.

Wright, Guy. (1981). "Why do Sealers Seal? Cultural Versus Economic Reasons for Participating in the Newfoundland Seal Hunt." *Culture* 1(1): 61–5.

Zilio, Michelle. (2013). "Inuit Groups and Sealers Lose Appeal to Overturn EU Seal Ban." *iPolitics,* April 25. https://ipolitics.ca/news/inuit-groups-and-sealers-lose -appeal-to-overturn-eu-seal-ban.

Interview List (all interviews conducted by the author)

Interview with Anne Troake, documentary filmmaker, October 27, 2022.

Interview with Faiza Outahsen, Greenpeace Netherlands, September 18, 2018.

Interview with James Winter, founding president of the Canadian Sealers Association, December 30, 2021.

Interview with Jessica Wilson, Greenpeace Canada, October 20, 2018.

Interview with Mads Flarup Christensen, Greenpeace Nordic, February 7, 2019.

Index